The Sabbath
Of The
Ten Commandments

Aubrey L. Duncan
Bridge To Life Ministries, Inc
Lithonia, GA

All Rights Reserved © 2006 by Aubrey L. Duncan
No part of this book may be reproduced or transmitted in any form
or by any means, graphic, electronic or mechanical, including photocopying,
recording, taping, or by any information storage retrieval
system, without the written permission of the publisher.

ISBN: 0-9749490-1-9

Published by
Bridge to Life Ministries, Inc.
P.O. Box 2106
Lithonia, GA 30058
(770) 908-3459

www.bridgetolife.net

Library of Congress Catalog Number 2006902253

Printed in the United States of America

When a man who is honestly mistaken

hears the truth,

he will either quit being mistaken

or cease to be honest…

Contents

Introduction..6

The Sabbath In Creation..12

The Sabbath And The Prophets 19

The Sabbath And Jesus..29

Sabbath Of The Ten Commandments......................................38

From Sabbath To Sunday..51

A Beast In History..67

Identifying The Beast And Its Mark..76

America And The Sabbath..92

The Sabbath And The Signs Of The Times 105

The Sabbath And The Ecumenical Movement......................123

Confronting Objections to The Sabbath................................129

Righteousness By Faith And The Sabbath.............................150

Some Thoughts On Keeping The Sabbath Holy....................160

Conclusion..167

Introduction

There is much confusion in the Christian world regarding the Sabbath. Some question which day is the Sabbath, while others claim it has been done away with. Yet others assert that the Sabbath was given to, and therefore was meant for the Jews only. There are those who proclaim that the Sabbath was nailed to the cross. Of course, there are those who teach that there are many Sabbaths. Views on the Sabbath are as varied as the number of those who advocate those views.

The purpose of this book is to focus on those views and to present the Biblical perspective on this vitally important and enduring doctrine. This volume will shed Biblical light on this quite controversial and critical subject. In fact, you will discover that, from a Biblical point of view, God's Sabbath is anything but controversial. Now, more than at any time in human history, the matter of the Sabbath and its place in everyone's life needs to be clearly understood by all.

It is hoped, that with a careful and prayerful study of this subject, hearts will be ennobled, thoughts will be refined, minds will be sharpened and the reader will be drawn into a closer relationship with our Lord and Savior, Jesus Christ.

As you look at the Sabbath from creation through redemption, you will discover that this is a matter dearly close to the heart of God. Your heart will be touched to realize that the Sabbath is more than a pause in time in which a prescribed set of rites and rituals must be followed. Quite to the contrary, you will be delighted to learn that the Sabbath is an inestimable gift from our Creator...a gift to be honored and cherished by all.

Like all the other spiritual gifts God has given to us, He wants us not only to keep the Sabbath in this life, but also to possess it through redemption and eternity.

INTRODUCTION

The apostle Paul declares, "...For though there be that are called gods, whether in heaven or in earth, (as there be gods many, and lords many)... But to us there is but one God, the Father, of whom are all things, and we in Him; and one Lord Jesus Christ, by whom are all things, and we by Him..." (1 Corinthians 8: 5,6). Likewise, though there be various Sabbaths so called, there is but one Sabbath. It is the Sabbath of the Lord...the seventh day Sabbath.

Our Lord and Savior, Jesus Christ, epitomizes this enduring Biblical truth. As we come to find rest in Him, we will realize that the Sabbath-rest is the greatest evidence of our obedience to Him, and trust in Him as our creator and redeemer.
Paul teaches us, "...But without faith it is impossible to please Him: for He that cometh to God must believe that He is, and that He is the rewarder of them that diligently seek Him...." (Hebrews 11:6). He continues, as he quotes the prophet Habakkuk,"...For therein is the righteousness of God revealed from faith to faith: as it is written 'The just shall live by faith...' (Romans 1:17).

The Christian life is one of faith. Everything that we believe, teach and live must be based on faith. That faith is established upon the word of God. Faith means believing in God. It is trusting, without doubt, what He has revealed in His word. Christianity is rooted and grounded in that faith. Since none of us were there when God created the world, or when Christ was born, died on Calvary and rose from the dead; and since none of us were eyewitnesses to the marvelous events of Scripture, then we must conclude that it is by faith alone that we live and have our being.

And what is that faith? Paul again teaches,"...Now faith is the substance of things hoped for, the evidence of things not seen..." (Hebrews 11:1). This faith is an abiding trust in, and total commitment to God's word. Regardless of any man's opinion or our own personal feelings, genuine faith demands our yielding to God's word and God's word only. Such faith comes ONLY by a personal, dedicated study of God's word. Hence, Paul declares, "...So then, faith cometh by hearing, and hearing by the word of God...." (Romans 10:17).

As you approach this study on God's Sabbath, it is only with this faith that the right conclusions can be drawn and the correct decision arrived at. It is the sincere prayer of this writer that the right decision will be made by the reader. It is faith and faith alone that can enlighten sinful man to the things of a sinless, infinite God. Education won't do it. Scholarly theology doesn't achieve it. Intellectual philosophy can't arrive at it. Not only are we saved by faith, but we are also spiritually enlightened by it. We live by it. We grow with it. We will ultimately be delivered by it.

The Sabbath therefore, like all of God's revelations to us, is a matter of faith. As we look unto Jesus, the author and finisher of our faith, we observe that He, above all men, kept the Sabbath in highest regard. He did not, as some teach, break the Sabbath. Had He done so, He would be just like us, a lost sinner. Consequently, He could in no wise have been our Savior. Ultimately, it is to Him that we look as we seek to understand and settle this issue of God's Sabbath in our hearts.

The word "**Sabbath**" means rest. It is a Hebrew word transferred into the English language. When the Hebrews used the word "**Sabbath**", it conveyed the same idea to them that the word "rest" does to us. The fourth commandment therefore really says to us, "…Remember the **rest** day, to keep it holy. Six days shall thou labor, and do all thy work: But the seventh day is the rest of the Lord thy God: in it thou shall not do any work, thou, nor thy son, nor thy daughter, thy manservant, nor thy maidservant, nor thy cattle, nor thy stranger that is within thy gates: For in six days the Lord made heaven and earth, the sea, and all that in them is, and rested the seventh day: wherefore the Lord blessed the **rest** day, and hallowed it…." (Exodus 20:8-11)

We must not make the mistake of judging the Lord's rest for what men are accustomed to call rest. God is not a man. We should rather learn from God's rest, what rest really is. God'srest is not mere physical rest from weariness. This we know from two facts. First, "…God is spirit, and they that worship Him must worship Him in spirit and in truth…" (John 4:24) Not "a spirit," as though He were one of many; but He is Spirit. Second, "…The everlasting God, the Lord, the Creator of the ends of the earth, faint not, neither is weary…" (Isaiah 40:28.)

INTRODUCTION

His rest is not physical, but spiritual. Since He is Spirit. God rested not because He was weary, but because His work of creation was finished. He thus used the concept of rest to signify His completed work of creation. When work is finished, and it is well done, nothing but rest remains. In six days, God finished His work. As He surveyed it, He pronounced it, "very good." There was no flaw in it. It was without fault before Him. Therefore, since God's work was done and well done at the close of the sixth day, "...He rested on the seventh day from all the work which He had made..." (Genesis 2:1, 2) He had no sad reflections. There were no regrets. His rest was not marred. It was not what man calls rest. It implied no such thoughts as, "...Tomorrow I must go at that work again" nor "I wish I had done this portion a little differently" nor "If I could do that over again, I could make an improvement" nor "That last day's work is so bad that I cannot bear to look at it" nor "I was so tired when I got to it that I couldn't half do it" Rest for God is nothing of the kind. Every portion of God's work, even mankind, was as perfect as it could possibly be. God took divine delight in contemplating the work from which He was resting, because it was complete and perfect. This is the rest that He offers to us. It is not something he imposes upon us; but which He, in everlasting love and kindness, gives freely to us. The Sabbath-rest is not a task that is laid upon one. It is not a burden. Those who look upon the Sabbath as a burden have no idea of what God's Sabbath is. It is rest -perfect, unalloyed rest.

Jesus Christ is the One who made the worlds. "...For by Him were all things created, that are in the heaven,and that are in the earth, visible and invisible, whether there be thrones, or dominions, or principalities, or powers: all things were created by Him, and for Him..." (Colossians 1:16)

Therefore, He is the One who offers us this rest. To every soul, Jesus lovingly pleads, "...Come unto me, all ye that labor and are heavy laden, and I will give you rest..." (Matthew 11:28) Rest is found in Him. In Him the works of God are completed. In Him is the new creation. The apostle Paul tells us: "...if anyman be in Christ, he is a new creature..." (2 Corinthians 5:17)

On the cross Jesus cried, "...It is finished..." (John 19:30). Jesus thus showing that in His cross we find the perfect rest that comes only from the finished work of the Lord. This rest is gained by faith. Those who believe do enter into His rest. How so? By faith, we have the finished, perfect work of the Lord as our own, "…This is the work of God, that ye believe on Him whom He hath sent…" (John 6:29) Believing Him means obeying Him. Since in Him (Jesus Christ) the works of God are complete, it follows that by believing in Him we find the rest that God intends for us to have. The rest Jesus gives is rest from sin. The heavy-laden, whom He calls to Him, are those who are burdened with the weight of their sins. All men are thus burdened. "…For all have sinned and come short of the glory of God…" (Romans 3:23) Our best works are utterly worthless to gain God's favor. Nevertheless, Christ will have a people who are "…zealous of good works…" (Titus 2:14) The good works must be those that God Himself has wrought for us in Christ. Only His work is enduring. "…His work is honorable and glorious; and his righteousness endures forever…" (Psalm 111:3)

Therefore, Paul declares, "…by grace are ye saved through faith; and that not of yourselves; it is the gift of God; not of works, lest any man should boast. For we are his workmanship, created in Christ Jesus unto good works, which God hath before prepared that we should walk in them…" (Ephesians 2:8-10) It is: "…not by works done in righteousness, which we did ourselves, but according to His mercy He saved us, through the washing of regeneration and renewing of the Holy Ghost, which He shed on us abundantly, through Jesus Christ our Savior…" (Titus 3:5,6)

It is by the works of God that we are saved, and not by our own. Good works there are in abundance. They are for us to do. But, through no work of our own are we saved. We are saved solely through faith in the perfect work of God through Jesus Christ. If the works were our own, then the rest would be our own. God gives us His rest, not ours. Only His works can yield perfect rest. He hath made His wonderful works. The memorial of that work is the seventh day. It is the day on which God rested from all His works. Moses records, "…And on the seventh day God ended His work which He had made, and rested on the seventh day from all His work which He had made…And God blessed the seventh day and sanctified it: because that in it He had rested from all His work which God had created and made.." (Genesis 2:2,3)

The seventh day is God's Sabbath. That is the day He has blessed, sanctified and made holy. Its holiness has never departed from it. Whatsoever

God doeth, is shall be forever. No matter what man does, nor how man regards the day, its holiness remains. It is still holy and sanctified. No man can alter that fact. Paul again declares: "...For if Jesus hath given them rest, then would He not have spoken of another day ...There remains therefore a rest for the people of God..." (Hebrews 4:8,9)

The seventh day, which God forever declares to be His rest, is the means by which He shows us, the perfection of His creation. The Sabbath calls on us to contemplate a finished and perfect new creation. It reveals to us the everlasting God, the unwearied, almighty Creator, "... who has wrought and laid up great goodness for them that trust in Him before the sons of men..." (Psalm 31:19).

The seventh-day Sabbath reminds us that we are complete in Him, who is the head of all principality and power. It tells us that, although we have sinned, and brought the curse upon God's perfect creation; the cross of Christ, which bears the curse, restores and perpetuates the perfect work of God. Through it, we may stand without fault before the throne of God, just as when man was first made. This is the Sabbath which this study will help you to understand.

Thanks be to God for His unspeakable gift.

CHAPTER 1
The Sabbath In Creation

As we embark upon this study of the Sabbath, our first duty is to determine the origin of the Sabbath. There is but one place where we can discover the origin of God's Sabbath. That place is in His word, the holy Bible. The apostle Paul, in writing to a young minister and fellow worker in the cause of Jesus Christ, admonishes Timothy, "…Study to show thyself approved unto God, a workman that need not to be ashamed, rightly dividing the word of truth…" (2 Timothy 2:15) In the same letter, Paul continues, "…And that from a child thou hast known the holy Scriptures, which are able to make thee wise unto salvation through faith which is in Christ Jesus… All scripture is given by inspiration of God, and is profitable for doctrine, for reproof, for correction, for instruction in righteousness…that the man of God may be perfect, thoroughly furnished unto all good works…" (2 Timothy 3:15-17)

It is by God's word, and God's word alone, that we can arrive at the right conclusions in our Christian experience. This is where we begin our study of the Sabbath…in the word of God.

From the very beginning of the Holy Scriptures, we are confronted with the subject of faith. Moses declares,"…In the beginning God created the Heaven and the earth…" (Genesis 1:1) He gives no preamble. No philosophical dissertation is presented. No theological exegesis is entered into. He simply gives us an unambiguous declaration of who God is…our Creator. Do you believe this?

If, by faith, you believe this assertion, then you must also believe everything else that follows. This declaration, like all of Scripture, demands our unyielding faith. The Genesis narrative continues in a profoundly systematic way. It unfolds the acts and deeds of an omniscient, all-powerful God, as He creates everything out of nothing.

God is unapologetically self-assertive in His revelation to us about His creation. He declares not only who He is, but also what He does.

The record reveals that out of that nothingness, our God first created the night and the day. The night, being the first part, preceding the light part called the day. Together He pronounced them the first day. As of the time you are reading this book, nothing has changed. The night still exists followed by the day. The God who created it still exists. Unless you are an atheist, who does not believe in God, your faith demands that He (God) still exists, even as the day which He created also exists.

God revealed to Moses His creation of the second day. God continued with the work of creation. He (God) called into existence the heavens and the waters of the oceans. Moses recorded that the evening, (the dark part of day) and the morning, (the light part) was the second day (Genesis 1:6-8) We still have the night and the day. We also still have the heavens and the oceans.

The Supreme Master Builder proceeded to enhance His work of creation. He revealed to Moses what He did on the third day. He called forth the earth out of the waters. He created not just the earth; but God dressed it and beautified it with luscious green grass, lilies, roses and other flowers, innumerable in quantity and unspeakable in beauty. The vegetation and the foliage He also called forth. He declared them perfect and good. Moses recorded that this was the third day (the evening and the morning), (Genesis 1:11-13), but, God was not quite done.

He proceeded to illuminate the heavens with the moon, the stars and the sun. Not only were these heavenly bodies for beautification; but, inspiration revealed that God ordained them to be for times and seasons. God delegated the moon and stars to the night (the dark part of day) and relegated the sun to the day (the bright part) He thus provided for man a means of measuring the days, the seasons and years. This was God's doing, not man's. We are utterly incapable of creating time. Therefore, it is impossible for man to change time. We cannot alter the amount of time that God has given us. Moses declared that this was the fourth day (the evening and the morning) (Genesis 1:14-19). God's plan moved on. He then created the animals of the earth, the fish of the seas (waters) and the birds of the air (the firmament). He created them as they were, to procreate their own kind (Genesis 1:20-25). This was the fifth day.

Notice here that God in His infinite wisdom, provided a dwelling place and sustenance for His creatures before He created them. The record does not indicate that any species evolved one from the other; but rather each came forth as God created it.

The process of creation revealed that God is a God of order and specificity. Everything not only fits where it is supposed to fit, but when it is supposed to fit.

This is the record. God created the night and day (first day). Then He created Heaven (second day). He proceeded to create the seas, the earth, vegetation and foliage (third day). God then created the moon, the stars and sun, (fourth day). He then called forth the animals, the birds and the fish (fifth day).

Thus the heavens and the earth were completed except for His greatest creation of all, man. This God did on the sixth day. But what is man? The Psalmist David answers, "...What is man, that thou art mindful of him, and the son of man that thou visited him? For thou hast made him a little lower than the angels and has crowned him with glory and honor...Thou made him to have dominion over the works of thine hands; thou hast put all things under his feet..." (Psalms 8:4-6)

The glory and honor with which man was crowned at creation is God's. The record reveals that God created man in God's own image, (Genesis 1:27). Adam, the first man, and Eve, the first woman had the virtues and characteristics of God. They were loving, truthful, honest, meek, peaceful, gentle, temperate, obedient and faithful. They were perfect in their ways before God. Man was given authority over all that was created before him, (Genesis 1:28). All were created for man's benefit. They were gifts from God. All of God's creations were good and beneficial to man for some aspect of his life. (Genesis 1:26-31)

Of all of God's creations, only the creation of man provides some detail as to how He(God) created him. Of the other creations, the record simply declares, "God created." But for man, Moses writes, "...And the Lord God formed man from the dust of the ground, and breathed into his nostrils the breath of life; and man became a living soul..." (Genesis 2:7).

Notice that man became a living soul. He was not gifted with an immortal soul. God also provided (for man) one to complement him and be a helper to him. Moses again writes, "...and the Lord God said, it is not good that the man should be alone. I will make him an helpmeet for him...And the Lord God caused a deep sleep to fall upon Adam; and he slept. And He (God) took one of his (Adam's) ribs, and closed up the flesh thereof; and the rib, which the Lord God had taken from the man, made He a woman and brought her unto the man..." (Genesis 2:18, 21, 22)

Thus God established the first human family. It consisted of one man and one woman, bound together by God, their creator. His command to them was to procreate after their kind (Genesis 1:28). The institution of marriage was herewith established.

God, having created the heaven and the earth, the sea and all that are in them, and man to have authority and dominion over them, declared it all to be perfect. This was on the sixth day (evening and morning) (Genesis 1:31).

The work of creation now completed in six days, God bequeaths to man an inestimable gift. Moses declares, "...Thus the heavens and the earth were finished, and all the host of them...And on the seventh day, God ended His work which He had made and rested on the seventh day, from all His work which He had made...And God blessed the seventh day, and sanctified it; because in it He had rested from all His work which God created and made..." (Genesis 2:1-3)

If you have read this far and if you believe what you have read, then you must agree that it is by faith that we must accept this record. The man of God, Paul, declares, "...we walk by faith and not by sight..." (2 Corinthians. 5:7) Faith demands that we accept the creation record. There is no other basis on which we may or can accept it. As one reviews the record of creation, it is inescapable that God has provided all things that He created for man's enjoyment, wellness and nourishment. With your faith, hopefully still intact, let us take a closer look at the Sabbath in creation.

As was already stated in the introductory chapter of this book, the word 'Sabbath' is simply a Hebrew language translation for the word 'rest'. Of the seven days of the week, God chose one, the seventh-day, as a day of rest. God did not choose any one of the seven, nor did He designate the first; but rather, most specifically the Scripture states that God chose the seventh-day as His day of rest. This rest was not for God's benefit. God does not need rest like we do. The record simply expresses the thought that God's work of creation was completed in six days. The seventh day He has set apart from the other days as holy, blessed and sanctified. It is esteemed in a way the other six are not.

The creation of God lasts forever. Today, there is no denying that we have day and night. No one says that there is no heaven, earth nor seas. It is impossible to say that the trees, flowers and vegetation are nonexistent. And what of the animals, the birds and fish? They are still here with us. The moon, the stars and the sun still bless us with their radiance and provide the only reliable measure of times, seasons and years. And man, what about him? We are still here. All this is not by chance.

The apostate prophet Balaam certainly understood the concept of God's immutable, irreversible acts. He declared, "…how shall I curse whom God has not cursed? And how shall I defile whom the Lord hath not defiled… Behold, I have received commandment to bless and He had blessed, and I cannot reverse it…" (Numbers 23:8,20) So it is with all of God's creation. He has created it and no man can un-create it. The seventh-day Sabbath, as part of that creation, cannot be undone by anyone. No man, no ecclesiastical council or philosopher can un-bless, un-create or deny that which God has created, blessed and sanctified. The sacred Scriptures continue, "…Now therefore let it please thee to bless the house of thy servant, that it may be before thee forever. For thou blessed, O Lord, and it shall be blessed forever…" (1 Chronicles 17:27)

What God blesses, He blesses forever. He blessed and sanctified the Sabbath-day and it is thus blessed forever. There is no record of God removing his blessing from the Sabbath, or doing away with it from His creation.

Some may attempt to deny it, but the Sabbath is still blessed and sanctified. You may trample upon it by doing your own work on it, but it is still holy. Man may attempt to change it, but the seventh-day Sabbath remains hallowed.

Though unconverted hearts proclaim that the Sabbath is done away with, the Sacred record plainly states that it is created forever and thus blessed forever. God has blessed the Sabbath and it is forever blessed. Yet others deceptively declare that the Sabbath day is for the Jews. There were no Jews at creation.

There is no such mention in the record of creation. Rather, our Creator and Savior declares, "…The Sabbath was made for man, and not man for the Sabbath…" (Mark 2:27). That is exactly what the Sabbath is, a gift from God to all mankind.

How could any man, claiming to be a child of God, name the name of Christ and yet deny the Sabbath? To reject the Sabbath is to reject one of the most precious gifts from God. To reject His gift is to reject Him. Regardless of what pretext one uses to cast aside the Sabbath; what they are in fact doing is turning away from the God of creation. He gave us the Sabbath as an eternal sign of His creative power.

God, in His mercy and love for us, sends out a love message to all mankind in these times in which we live."…Fear God and give glory to Him; for the hour of His judgment is come; and worship Him that made heaven and earth, and the sea, and the fountains of waters…" (Rev. 14:7) This is a warning message.

It announces to the world that God's final judgment has begun. He (God) calls all men back to worship Him as creator. And how do we show the world that we worship the true God, Creator of the heaven and the earth? By accepting His gift of rest in Him given at creation. We recognize and uplift the sign of His creatorship. It is not only for the Jews, as some men claim, but for all mankind. That gift, that sign is His holy and blessed Sabbath day.

If by faith, we accept the works of creation, then by faith, we must also accept the 'rest' of creation. A life of work without rest is a life of pain, heartache and misery. Such is a life of no peace. It is a life constantly seeking to find that which God has already given us from creation, the peace and rest of His blessed Sabbath day. What child of God would want to deny, reject and cast aside such peace and rest?

The Sabbath, from God's perspective, is not so much about what we do or do not do on the seventh day. It is not about an endless set of rules, rites and rituals. Rather, the Sabbath is a time for us to reflect upon and recognize the manifold blessings God has provided for us during the previous six days. It is a place in time made holy by the One who blesses us abundantly. The Sabbath is a time in which we may rest from our toils and secular labors to contemplate and appreciate all that God has done for us. The Sabbath, ultimately, is an eternal footnote of the unbounded goodness of our Creator. It is a time of reflection during which we focus upon His matchless blessings towards us. It is the seventh day of the week, now called Saturday.

Moses and the prophets of old recognized this inescapable fact. In our next chapter, we will take an inspired look at how some of God's prophets regarded and related to the Sabbath.

Chapter 2
The Sabbath and The Prophets

In the previous chapter, it was plainly established that it is God who gave the Sabbath to mankind. We found out that He bestowed it to us as a gift. This gift, like all other gifts from God, is for our edification and His glorification. The Sabbath, therefore, is to us a precious treasure and an eternal emblem by which we may always remember who is our Creator. It affords us rest from our labors. It is a time when we may come apart, contemplate His great works of creation (themselves, priceless gifts to us) and appreciate His manifold blessings to us.

We also discovered, in the last chapter, that whatsoever God blesses, He blesses forever and no man can curse or change. Our Lord and Savior Jesus Christ, the expressed image of God (Hebrews 1:3), is declared by the apostle Paul, to be also changeless. Under the inspiration of the Holy Spirit, Paul writes, "…Jesus Christ the same yesterday, and today, and forever…" (Hebrews 13:8).

It therefore follows that with respect to the Sabbath, God having created it, He would continue to impress it upon the hearts of men. And how does He do this? The apostle Paul answers, "…God who at sundry times and in divers manners spoke in times past unto the fathers by the prophets…" (Hebrews 1:1) But who are the prophets and what did they have to say about the Sabbath? These questions we will answer in this chapter.

As we proceed, we must remember that our walk is one of faith. Therefore, all that we present is based solely on faith in God's word. As men of God, the prophets delivered the word of God. Peter declares, "…For the prophecy came not in old time by the will of man, but holy men of God spoke as they were moved by the Holy Ghost..." (1 Peter 1:21) This fact is likewise established by Samuel, the prophet. He writes, "...Beforetime in Israel, when a man went to inquire of God, thus he spoke, come and let us go to the Seer: for he that is now called a Prophet was before time called a Seer..." (1 Samuel 9:9)

The life of a prophet of God is always in conformity with God's will. His/her work is to comfort God's people when they hurt and to correct them when they are going down the wrong path. The prophet also confirms God's people when they are walking in the right way. The counsel of the prophet is always to direct men's hearts towards God and His requirements for their lives. He or she does not speak contrary to the word of God. Isaiah declared,"...To the law and to testimony, if they speak not according to this word, it is because there is no light in them..." (Isaiah 8:20) We are admonished: "...believe in the Lord your God so shall ye be established; believe his prophets, so shall ye prosper..." (2 Chronicles 20:20). With this understanding of who are the prophets, let us examine what they taught about God's Sabbath.

For some time after the creation record, no mention is made of the Sabbath. We next encounter the Sabbath when the prophet Moses is accused of giving his people rest from their labors. He was determined to forsake the fame and fortune of Egyptian royalty to dwell and suffer with his people, the Hebrew slaves of Egyptian captivity. The record reveals, "...And Pharaoh said, Behold the people of the land now are many, and ye (Moses) make them to rest from their burdens..." (Exodus 5:5).

As was explained earlier, the word Sabbath is translated to mean rest. Therefore, it is safe to conclude, that within the context of this narrative, the rest mentioned is the Sabbath. Further evidence in this regard is established as we follow the Israelites in their wilderness wanderings. We later find that the people of God, having been delivered from Egyptian bondage, are again instructed to keep holy God's Sabbath-day.

The Hebrews, as they journeyed through the wilderness, had the high privilege of being fed by God with food that descended from on high. The heavenly food, called Manna, (Exodus 16:31) was miraculously rained down from Heaven for six days a week. For five days, just enough to feed the people for each day, was provided.

But on the sixth day, the Scripture declares, "...and it came to pass that on the sixth day they gathered twice as much bread (manna), two omens for one man: and all the rulers of the congregation came and told Moses ... and he said unto them: this is that which the Lord hath said, tomorrow is the rest of the holy Sabbath unto the Lord: bake that which ye shall today: and seethe that ye will seethe: and that which remained over, lay up for you to be kept until the morning. And they laid it up till the morning, as Moses bade and it did not stink, neither was there any worm therein ... And Moses said, eat that today, for today is a Sabbath unto the Lord: today ye shall not find it in the field ... Six days ye shall gather it: but on the seventh day, which is the Sabbath, in it there shall be none..." (Exodus 16:22-26)

The Sabbath, which God gave at creation, is here being clearly referred to by Moses, God's prophet. He (Moses) reiterates, "...See, for that the Lord hath given you the Sabbath, therefore He gave you on the sixth day the bread of two days; abide ye every man in his place, let no man go out of his place on the seventh day..." (Exodus 16:29)

As God's prophet, Moses recognized the importance of following the will of God. God had revealed to Moses that from creation, the seventh-day Sabbath was a matter of deepest importance to His people. Moses therefore kept it constantly before the people's mind. God ensured that by the miracle of the manna, the Sabbath truth would be impressed upon the hearts of the people.

Of such importance is the Sabbath to God that upon giving to Moses His moral Law, God included Sabbath keeping as one of His holy Commandments. The record reads, "...Remember the Sabbath day to keep it holy, six days shall thou labor and do all thy work; but the seventh day is the Sabbath of the Lord thy God; in it thou shall not do any work, thou nor thy son, nor thy daughter, nor thy manservant, nor thy maidservant, nor thy cattle, nor thy stranger that is within thy gates ... For in six days the Lord made the heaven and the earth, the sea and all that in them is, and rested the seventh day; wherefore God blessed the Sabbath day and hallowed it (made it holy)" (Exodus 20:8-11)

The God who never changes, is forever reminding His people,

through His prophet Moses, of the significance of His seventh-day Sabbath. The command directs the mind back to the One who is the Creator. He has not ceased from being our Creator. Therefore, it is ludicrous to suggest that His creatures can cast aside His Sabbath, which is the sign of His creatorship. Moses reminded God's people, "…Six days may work be done: but in the seventh is the Sabbath of rest, holy to the Lord: whosoever doeth any work in the Sabbath day, he shall surely be put to death … wherefore the children of Israel shall keep the Sabbath, to observe the Sabbath throughout their generations, for a perpetual covenant … It is a sign between Me (God) and the children of Israel forever: for in six days the Lord made heaven and earth, and on the seventh day He rested and was refreshed…" (Exodus 31:15-17) Again, we find the Sabbath a reminder of who is the Creator.

One may be quick to say, 'But that was for Israel of old, as the Scripture says, and is not binding on us Christians today'. Let us now examine that charge.

Quite correctly, this commandment was given through Moses for the children of Israel. But the question must be asked, 'Who is Israel?' The apostle Paul answers plainly, "…For he is not a Jew, which is one outwardly; neither is that circumcision. But he is a Jew, which is one inwardly and circumcision is that of the heart, in the Spirit, and not in the letter; whose praise is not of men, but of God …" (Romans 2:28, 29)

A Jew is simply one who acknowledges the God of creation as the only true God and demonstrates faith in His word by the keeping of all His commandments.

The term **Jew'** denotes both a nation and a religion. God established that nation and religion through His servant Abraham. The record reveals that God spoke to Abraham thus, "…And I will make of thee a nation, and I will bless thee and make thy name great; and thou shall be a blessing. And I will bless them that bless thee; and curse them that curse thee; and in thee shall all the nations of the earth be blessed…" (Genesis 12:2 & 3)

Despite Abraham's and his wife Sarah's old age, and their apparent inability to bear a child, let alone produce a nation, the

Scriptures declare, "...And he (Abraham) believed in the Lord and He counted it to him for righteousness..." (Genesis 15:6, Roman 4:3) The record continues, "...Because that Abraham obeyed my voice, and kept my charge, my commandments, my statutes and my laws..." (Genesis 26:5)

The Jewish nation was thus established. Because of his faith in the word of the Lord, Abraham became the father of the Jews. He is the father of the faithful. Paul concurs, "...and he (Abraham) received the sign of circumcision, a seal of the righteousness of the faith which he had yet being uncircumcised; that he might be the father of all them that believe, though they be not circumcised; that righteousness may be imputed unto them also ..." (Romans 4:11).

The name **Israel** was accorded the Jews as a result of Jacob, Abraham's grandson, who had a change of heart and a name change from Jacob to Israel. Moses again writes, "...And He (God) said, Thy name shall be called no more Jacob, but **Israel:** for as a prince hast thou power with God and with men and has prevailed..." (Genesis 32:28). Through Jacob's twelve sons, great tribes were established. In time, they came to be known as the tribes or the children of Israel. Hence, Moses in Exodus chapter 31:15 & 16(quoted earlier) refers to God's people as Israel. The title refers to those who have experienced the transforming power of the Creator.

Israel is a spiritual term. It defines those, who through faith in the God of creation, overcome cultivated and hereditary sin. The term today is much misused and misapplied.

The question now is, 'do you have faith in God?' If you do, then you, according to Paul, are a Jew. You are Israel. Paul sums it up thus, ".... So then, they which be of faith are blessed with faithful Abraham " (Galatians 3:9). He continues, "...There is neither Jew nor Greek, there is neither bond nor free, there is neither male nor female: for we are all one in Christ Jesus... And if ye be Christ's then are ye Abraham's seed, and heirs according to the promise..." (Galatians 3:28-29)

Now, if you claim Jesus Christ as your Savior, you are indeed a Jew and an Israelite. By faith you are. Therefore, the Sabbath of creation is for you. The Sabbath that Moses reminded the people of God to keep holy is yours also. If you claim to be an heir to the promise, then you must also abide by the commandments that come with the promise. Our relationship with God is a covenant relationship. God extends His mercy and grace to us. He provides for us His laws. He requires and empowers us to obey. We agree to keep His laws.

It is that simple. It is that plain. Following the example and admonitions of Moses, the people of God held fast to the Sabbath. They recognized its significance and importance in their lives. When they neglected to honor the Sabbath, peril and destruction always followed. The prophets of God, who came after Moses, likewise admonished the nation of Israel to hold the Sabbath in the highest esteem God intended it to be. The prophet Jeremiah, recognizing the evil that was to befall the people of God, if they continue to defile the Sabbath, warned, "…Thus says the Lord: take heed to yourselves and bear no burden on the Sabbath day, nor bring it in by the gates of Jerusalem neither carry forth a burden out of your houses on the Sabbath day, neither do ye any work, but hallow ye the Sabbath day, as I commanded your fathers…" (Jeremiah 17:21 & 22)

He further promised them that blessings would come upon them if they keep the Sabbath holy as God intended them to. He continued: "…And it shall come to pass, if ye diligently harken unto me, says the Lord, to bring in no burden through the gates of this city on the Sabbath-day, but hallow the Sabbath-day, to do no work therein…Then shall there enter into the gates of the city, kings and princes sitting upon the throne of David, riding on chariots and horses, they and their princes, the men of Judah and the inhabitants of Jerusalem, and this city shall remain forever, and they shall come from the cities of Judah, and from the places about Jerusalem, and from the land of Benjamin, and from the plain, and from the mountains, and from the south, bringing burnt offerings, and sacrifices, and meat offerings, and incense, and bringing sacrifices of praise, unto the house of the Lord…" (Jeremiah 17: 25,26). Such are the blessings of keeping God's Sabbath holy.

Jeremiah concluded by pronouncing the evil that will befall the people if they refused to obey God's command in keeping the Sabbath-day holy. He warned the people on behalf of God, "…But if ye will not hearken unto me to hallow my Sabbath-day, and not to bear a burden, even entering into the gates of Jerusalem on the Sabbath-day, then will I kindle a fire in the gates thereof, and it will devour the palaces of Jerusalem, and it shall not be quenched." (Jeremiah 17:27)

Of course, the people did not listen to and obey the word of God sent through His prophet Jeremiah. The result was catastrophic. Jeremiah again prophesized, "…Behold, I will send and take all the families of the north said the Lord, and Nebuchadnezzar, the king of Babylon, my servant, and will bring them against this land and against the inhabitants thereof, and against all these nations round about and will utterly destroy them, and make them an astonishment and an hissing and perpetual desolations…" (Jeremiah 25:9)

With uncanny accuracy and divine precision, as a consequence of the Israelites dishonoring God's Sabbath, King Nebuchadezzar came down from Babylon, took God's people captive and scattered them throughout his empire. The record reveals, "…Therefore He (God) brought upon them the king of the Chaldees (Babylon) who slew their young men with the sword in the house of the sanctuary and had no compassion upon young man or maiden, old men, or him that stopped for age: He (God) gave them all into his (Nebuchadnezzar's) hand…" (2 Chronicles 36:17)

But God remained a God that does not change. Even in Babylonian captivity, He raised up a prophet to proclaim the sacredness of His Sabbath to His people. The prophet Ezekiel proclaimed from Babylonian captivity, "…Thus says the Lord God: the gate of the inner court that looks toward the east shall be shut six working days: but on the Sabbath it shall be opened…" (Ezekiel 46:1) The God of creation, who bequeathed to man His Sabbath from the beginning, has never, under any circumstances, relieved man from the obligation of keeping His Sabbath-day holy. This is so that men may forever remember who is the Creator.

It is the work of our adversary, the devil, to attempt by any means necessary, to blot out the memory of the Sabbath from men's hearts. This would lead them to forget their Creator and deny Him the worship that He alone deserves. But God is all-powerful. He ensures that in all ages, under all circumstances, He will have prophets. He inspires them to turn men's heart back to their Creator. The prophets do so by uplifting the sanctity of the Sabbath before His people.

Thus Nehemiah was raised up. Having been sometime in Babylonian captivity, Nehemiah along with the Jewish nation was liberated. Precisely as God had prophesied, the declaration to set Israel free came in 536BC by the hands of Cyrus, king of Persia. Though some chose to remain in the Babylonian empire, many, including the prophet Nehemiah, took advantage of the opportunity to return to Jerusalem. God's people, as prophesied, were now liberated.

Nehemiah the prophet returned to Jerusalem some time later with a company to rebuild the temple. Upon arrival in Jerusalem, the prophet declared, "…Thou (God) came down also upon mount Sinai, and spoke with them from heaven, and gave them right judgments, and true laws, good statutes and commandments … And made known to them thy holy Sabbath and commanded them precepts, statutes and laws, by the hand of Moses, thy servant …" (Nehemiah 9:13,14). What a reminder to God's people.

Of all the statutes, laws, precepts and commandments mentioned by Nehemiah, only the Sabbath is specifically stated. Why so? Because the Sabbath directed their minds back to their Creator. Nehemiah continued to remind God's people, "…And if the people of the land bring ware or any victuals on the Sabbath-day to sell, then we would not buy it of them on the Sabbath-day, or on the holy day…" (Nehemiah 10:31)

Nehemiah's work of restoration of the Sabbath to God's people continued incessantly. He admonished Israel, "…In those days saw I in Judah some treading winepresses on the Sabbath, and bringing in sheaves and lading asses; as also wine, grapes and figs, and all manner of burdens, which they brought in Jerusalem on the Sabbath-day: and I testified against them in the day wherein they sold victuals, then I contended with the nobles of Judah, and said unto them, what evil thing is this that ye do and profane the Sabbath-day? Did not your fathers thus, and did not our God bring all this evil upon us, and upon this city? Yet ye bring more wrath upon Israel by profaning the Sabbath…"

(Nehemiah 13:15,17,18).

    The prophet pointed out to the people the seriousness of breaking and profaning God's holy Sabbath-day. It is no less so for us today. The prophet then turned his focus to the religious leaders, calling upon them to be living examples to the people. Nehemiah strongly admonished the leaders, "...And I commanded the Levites that they should cleanse themselves, and that they should come and keep the gates, to sanctify the Sabbath-day. Remember, O my God, concerning this also, and spare me according to the greatness of Thy mercy..." (Nehemiah 13:24)

    So also it is today. God, through His chosen vessels, is calling his people, particularly the religious leaders, to take a stand for Him. In the face of many challenges and proliferation of erroneous doctrines concerning the Sabbath, God is calling upon the religious leaders to return to Him by keeping His Sabbath-day holy and teaching their followers to do likewise.

    Of all the Old Testament prophets, none spoke of the benefits of the Sabbath to mankind like the Prophet Isaiah. He promised, "...Thus says the Lord, keep ye judgment, and do justice, for my salvation is near to come... Blessed is the man that doeth this, and to son of man that lay hold on it; that keep the Sabbath from polluting it, and keep his hand from doing evil... and also the sons of the stranger that join themselves to the Lord, to serve Him and to love the name of the Lord to be His servants, everyone that keep the Sabbath from polluting it, and take hold of my covenant..." (Isaiah 56:2,6)

    The prophet declared that we are blessed when we come to the knowledge of keeping God's Sabbath-day holy. We are blessed by doing so simply because God, from the beginning, had blessed the Sabbath-day in a very special way. (Genesis 2:2,3) Isaiah, of course, was talking to the Jews of his time. But even then, he completely obliterated the misconceived notion that the Sabbath was just for the Jews. In verse six of Isaiah chapter 56, (quoted above) it is clearly shown that the Sabbath is not only for the Jews; but for all, then and now, who join themselves to God.

    The question is, 'are you joined to God?' If your answer is yes and you claim Jesus Christ as your Savior, then the Sabbath is for you. As a child of the living God, you are required to keep the Sabbath-day holy. He can give you His strength and power to enable you to obey Him.

Isaiah continued, "…If thou turn away thy foot from the Sabbath, from doing thy pleasure on My holy day, and call the Sabbath a delight, the holy of the Lord, honorable, and shall honor Him, not doing your own ways, nor doing your own pleasure, nor speaking your own words … then shall thou delight thyself in the Lord, and I will cause thee to ride upon the high places of the earth and feed thee with the heritage of Jacob, thy father: for the mouth of the Lord has spoken it…" (Isaiah 58:13 & 14)

What child of God would want to deny such a promise and reject such a blessing? Yet so many do. God says that they do so because of ignorance. The prophet Hosea speaks to this issue, "…My people are destroyed for lack of knowledge: because thou has rejected knowledge, I will also reject thee, that thou shall be no more a priest to me: seeing that thou hast forgotten the law of thy God, I will also forget thy children…" (Hosea 4:6)

It is a tragedy for those who claim to love God but reject the precious gift of His holy Sabbath-day. Such a condition is particularly troubling when it is so plainly stated in God's Holy word, the Bible, which is so readily and abundantly available.

Finally, the prophet Isaiah foretells our worship experience in eternity. "…And it shall come to pass that from one new moon to the other, and from one Sabbath to the other, shall all flesh come to worship before me, saith the Lord…" (Isaiah 66:23)

To reject the Sabbath today is to forfeit that blessing tomorrow. We have heard the prophets, God's chosen vessels, address the subject of the Sabbath. To a man, they all proclaim its sanctity, sacredness and its special place in God's heart and in His plan for our salvation.

In our next chapter, we will discover how the greatest prophet of them all, our Lord and Savior Jesus Christ, taught and lived regarding the Sabbath.

CHAPTER 3
The Sabbath and Jesus

The work of a prophet, as we have discovered, has always been to correct God's people and point them towards God. Also, their work involved comforting and consoling God's people when they are hurt and confirming their actions when they are on the right path. Not only were they teachers by expounding upon the word of God, but their lifestyles testified to their connection with God. At all times, during their ministry, prophets lived according to the word and will of God.

No one fulfilled such a mission more than our Lord and Savior Jesus Christ. He thus spoke of Himself, "… The Spirit of the Lord is upon me, because He hath anointed me to preach the gospel to the poor, He hath sent me to heal the broken-hearted, to preach deliverance to the captives and recovering of sight to the blind, to set at liberty them that are bruised…" (Luke 4:18)

Quite interestingly, it was on the Sabbath-day that Jesus chose to declare to the world who He was and what His mission involved. Such are the blessings of the Sabbath. The record reveals,"…And He (Jesus) came to Nazareth, where He had been brought up; and, as His custom was, He went into the synagogue on the Sabbath-day, and stood up for to read…" (Luke 4:16).

This record alone is evidence enough regarding Jesus' attitude towards the Sabbath. How men can conjecture that Jesus abolished the Sabbath is beyond reason and without Scriptural foundation.

Jesus, being his/her example, the committed Christian should do likewise in going to church on the Sabbath-day, in the company of their Savior.

The Scripture confirms that Jesus was a prophet. Moses

prophesied, "...The Lord thy God will rise up unto thee a Prophet ,from the midst of thee, of thy brethren, like unto me; unto Him ye shall hearken..." (Deuteronomy 18:15) Lest there be any misunderstanding as to whom that prophet would be, Stephen declared to the Pharisees: "...This is that Moses, which said unto the children of Israel, 'A prophet shall the Lord thy God raise up unto you of your brethren, like unto me, Him ye shall hear..." (Acts 7:37).

As a true witness for Jesus, Stephen, in speaking to those that were about to stone him to death, boldly proclaimed Jesus Christ to be the prophet that Moses prophesied about. The apostle John concurs. In referring to Jesus, he declared, "...Many of the people therefore when they heard this saying, said, Of a truth this is THE PROPHET ..." (John 7:40)

The apostle Peter declares that not only was Jesus a prophet, but that He is our example. Says he, "...For even hereunto were ye called, because Christ also suffered for us, leaving us an example that we should follow His steps..." (1 Peter 2:21). Aswe follow Jesus, through the dusty streets of Palestine, we will surely discover what He has left us as an example with regard to the Sabbath.

Our first encounter with Jesus, on the Sabbath-day, is found in the account of Jesus and His disciples being accused by the Pharisees of breaking the Sabbath. The incident, recorded in the gospels of Matthew, Mark and Luke, revolved around Jesus' disciples plucking corn to eat on the Sabbath-day. Matthew reports, "...At that time, Jesus went on the Sabbath day through the corn; and His disciples were an hungered, and began to pluck the ears of corn and to eat...But when the Pharisees saw it, they said unto Him, Behold thy disciples do that which is not lawful to do on the Sabbath day..." (Matthew 12:1,2)

In responding to their charge, Jesus reminded them of David and his men when they entered into the sanctuary and ate the shewbread, which was not 'lawful' for them to do. Jesus also reminded them of certain indiscretions of the ancient priests in carrying out their duties. His (Jesus) conclusion to the matter is recorded thus, "...But if ye had known what this means, I will have mercy and not sacrifice, ye would not have condemned the guiltless...For the Son of man is Lord even of the Sabbath day..." (Matthew 12:7,8)

First of all, Jesus was not the one who plucked the ears of corn. The Scripture is abundantly clear that it was his disciples. Secondly, Jesus declared them to be guiltless. For one to obtain food and eat on the Sabbath-day, if they are hungry, is not breaking the Sabbath. It is clear from the account in all three Gospels that Jesus and His disciples did not purposely go out on the Sabbath-day to pick corn in defiance of the commandment not to do any work on the Sabbath-day. In fact, it is obvious that they were in transit from one place to another. During that time, Jesus' disciples got hungry and proceeded to feed themselves. More importantly, Jesus used the occasion to expose the hypocrisy of the Pharisees in their exacting, non-biblical rules regarding the Sabbath. Had His disciples been wrong in their actions, Jesus would have been the first to rebuke them. He did so, on many other occasions, when they erred in His presence.

Note also that even if His disciples had erred, Jesus did not condemn them, but rather, extended mercy. Forgiveness for breaking the law is not the same as condoning one's breaking the law. Finally, and most importantly, Jesus declared that He is Lord of the Sabbath.

Nowhere in this episode did Jesus make the slightest reference to doing away with the Sabbath. He simply reinforced the principle that the Sabbath was still binding. He also declared that He is the Master of the Sabbath. The Savior further taught that He would forgive men if, in ignorance, they transgress the Sabbath or any other commandment.

As we follow Jesus, we find Him in the temple on yet another Sabbath-day. The example is again given that attending worship services on the Sabbath-day is what God requires of us. By the example of Jesus, and not the tradition of men we must order our lives. In doing His work of mercy for which He came, Jesus was accused of breaking the Sabbath. The record reads, "...And it came to pass also on another Sabbath, that He entered into the synagogue and taught, and there was a man whose right hand was withered. And the Scribes and the Pharisees watched him, whether He would heal on the Sabbath-day; that they may find an accusation against Him..." (Luke 6:6,7).

Jesus, perceiving their thoughts, posed the questions, "…What man shall there be among you that shall have one sheep, and if it fall into a pit on the Sabbath-day, will he not lay hold on it and lift it out? How much then is a man better than a sheep? Wherefore is it lawful to do well on the Sabbath days…" (Matthew 12:11-12).

Of course, the Scribes and Pharisees were dumbfounded and could not answer Him truthfully. If they did, they would have condemned themselves. They therefore kept their silence. Then Jesus, looking upon the man with the withered hand, declared: "…Stretch forth thy hand…" (Matthew 12:13). And He (Jesus) healed him.

Again, nowhere in this scenario, did Jesus say that the Sabbath was no longer in effect. He certainly did not indicate that it was in any way less binding upon men because He came. Quite to the contrary, He confirmed that not only is the Sabbath-day yet holy; but showed by example that it is lawful, in the eyes of God, to perform acts of mercy on the Sabbath day. As we continue our journey with the Savior, we find Him proclaiming the message of the Kingdom on the Sabbath-day, at church. And once again He encountered an opportunity for healing. The Scripture records, "…And He was teaching in one of the synagogues on the Sabbath…And behold, there was a woman which had a spirit of infirmity 18 years, and was bowed together, and could in no wise lift up herself… And when Jesus saw her, He called her to Him and said unto her, Woman, thou art loosed from thy infirmity…And He laid hands on her and immediately she was made straight…" (Luke 13:10-13).

The leader of the synagogue was filled with indignation. He thought that Jesus was breaking the Sabbath. This leader had the unmitigated gall to remind Jesus that God had given six days in which men should work, including performing acts of mercy, and no such thing should be done on the Sabbath day. To which Jesus replied, "…Thou hypocrite, doth not each one of you on the Sabbath loose his ox or his ass from the stall and lead him away to watering…And ought not this woman, being a daughter of Abraham, whom Satan had bound, lo, these 18 years be loosed from this bond on the Sabbath day…?" (Luke13: 15,16).

The Scribes and Pharisees were convicted and ashamed. They

could not, in good conscience, doubt His pronouncement or truthfully accuse Jesus of breaking the Sabbath. The lesson taught here is not that the Sabbath is eliminated or is otherwise abandoned, but rather, that the Sabbath is established by performing works of mercy on the Sabbath day.

Accompanying Jesus, again on the Sabbath-day, we remain with Him as He makes His way to church. On His way there Jesus encountered a crippled man. This man found it impossible .to get others to help him step into the pool of Bethesda.

It was the prevailing belief that if, at certain times, one steps into the pool, he would be healed. Jesus, upon seeing this man and the helpless condition in which he found himself, was moved with compassion. Jesus appealed to him, "…Wilt thou be made whole…?" (John 5:7). The crippled man, perhaps not realizing who it was that spoke to him, replied by recounting all the problems he was having in getting healed. To which Jesus responded, "…Rise, take up thy bed and walk…" (John 5:8)

Because it was on the Sabbath-day, the Jewish leaders were extremely angry with Jesus and sought to persecute Him and slander Him. They pursued Him relentlessly until they finally caught up with Him. Realizing their motives and reading the intents of their hearts, Jesus asked, "…Did not Moses give you the law, and yet none of you keep the law…I have done one work and ye all marveled… Moses therefore gave unto you circumcision (not because it is of Moses, but of the fathers) and ye on the Sabbath-day receive circumcision, that the Law of Moses should not be broken; are ye angry at me, because I have made a man every whit whole on the Sabbath-day… Judge not according to the appearance, but judge righteous judgment…" (John 7:19,21- 24) We are once more faced with a situation where Sabbath keeping is confirmed and uplifted by Jesus. He taught, by example, what is proper to do on the Sabbath-day.

Though many see these incidents as evidence not to keep God's Sabbath-day holy; Jesus, our Savior plainly demonstrated differently by His example and teaching. These encounters exemplify that we are to keep the Sabbath day holy. They help us to do so by giving us examples of what it is permissible to do on the Sabbath.

Jesus teaches us that it is right in the sight of God to do good on the Sabbath-day. In stark contrast to what false prophets and teachers advocate, Jesus does not teach that men should profane or otherwise do away with the Sabbath-day, simply because He came and died for us. Instead, He gave us many examples of how to keep the Sabbath-day holy. As He gazed down the highway of prophetic time and foresaw the destruction of His beloved city, Jerusalem, and the end of the world, Jesus warned, "…But pray ye that your flight be not in the winter, neither on the Sabbath-day…" (Matthew 24:20)

Here is the clearest indication that Jesus did not abolish the Sabbath. Rather, it is plainly presented that the Sabbath should be kept after His death, even to the end of time. Jesus, like the other prophets before and after Him, constantly kept the importance of the Sabbath before the people's eyes.

The Messiah demonstrated the sanctity of the Sabbath even in death. All four of the gospel writers, Matthew, Mark, Luke and John testify to this fact. They all are remarkably consistent in reporting the events of Jesus' death, burial and resurrection. This being the case, the mention of one such account will be sufficient to illustrate the point of Jesus' rest on the Sabbath, even in death.

Luke records thus, "…And that day was the preparation day, and the Sabbath drew on… And the women also, which came with Him from Galilee, followed after, and beheld the sepulchre, and how His body was laid…And they returned and prepared spices and ointments and rested the Sabbath day, according to the commandment…" (Luke 23:54-56)

Certainly, Jesus' disciples never gave any thought to the notion that because He was crucified, the Sabbath was abolished. Nowhere, in His three and one half years of earthly ,ministry, did Jesus address the issue of changing or abolishing the seventh-day Sabbath. As He laid in the grave on the Sabbath-day, His disciples honored Him by continuing to follow what He had taught them by example, i.e. that the Sabbath-day is holy and must be kept thus.

The sanctity of the Sabbath has never changed. We who claim to be followers of Jesus Christ must strive, by His grace, to do as He did in all areas of our lives, including keeping of the Sabbath-day holy. The apostle John cautions us, "...He that saith he abideth in Him, ought himself also so to walk, even as He walked..." (1 John 2:6) And how did Jesus walk in regards to the Sabbath-day? He honored it and kept it holy according to the commandment. So must we.

In all the examples cited in this chapter, regarding Jesus Christ's attitude toward the Sabbath, we are confronted with the facts of how Jesus perceived the Sabbath and how He reflected it in His personal life. For the Jews of Jesus' time, the Sabbath was a burden. It was a time to be rigidly observed by complying with a regimen of man-made rules, rituals and regulations.

That which God has given as a blessing at creation, man had corrupted by adding a multitude of unwarranted rites and unbiblical regulations, thus making it burdensome. Unfortunately, that's the legacy of the Sabbath that has been handed down through the ages. That is a false picture.

For Christians, the Sabbath-day is a reminder of who is their Creator. It is also a commemoration of who is their Redeemer. Our Creator and Redeemer is none other than Jesus Christ. Paul stresses to Titus, "...Who (Jesus Christ) gave himself for us, that He might redeem us from all iniquity and purify unto himself a peculiar people, zealous of good work..." (Titus 2:14)

Additionally, Paul declared to the Jews who had come to accept Jesus as their Lord and Savior, "...For He spoke in a certain place of the seventh-day on this wise, 'and God did rest on the seventh day from all His works... For if Jesus had given them rest, then would He not afterward have spoken of another day... There remains therefore a rest for the people of God..." (Hebrews 4:4, 8)

Our rest is in Jesus Christ. Keeping the Sabbath-day holy is an outward demonstration of our rest in Him. It is an honor, a joy and a privilege to do so. Sabbath keeping is what Our Lord taught by precept and example. It is a blessing. It is truthfully abiding in Jesus. It is being yoked up with Him.

To keep the Sabbath holy is to delight in Jesus Christ as our Creator, Savior and Redeemer. The Sabbath day is a commemoration of our rest in Jesus. It is a sign to the world that we are truly His.

Jesus, on His sojourn on this earth, taught how to truly keep the Sabbath-day holy. He continues to empower us to do so today. By His humanity He touched humanity. By His divinity He laid hold on the throne of God. As the son of man he taught us to obey. As the Son of God He gave us the power to obey.

When you are truly resting in Him, He will lead and empower you to keep holy His blessed Sabbath-day. You would come to realize that Sabbath keeping is not a mere round of rituals, encompassing a list of do's and don'ts. Instead, you will be a partaker of a joyous experience in He who is your Maker and your Redeemer. And who is He? John tells us, ,m"…In the beginning was the Word and the Word was with God and the Word was God… The same was in the beginning with God…all things were made by Him and without Him was not anything made that was made… In Him was life and the life was the light of men… And the light shined in darkness, and the darkness comprehended it not… And the Word was made flesh and dwelt among us (and we beheld His glory, the glory of the only begotten of the Father) full of grace and truth…" (John 1:1-5, 14).

Paul reminds us, "…God who at sundry times and in divers manners spoke in times past unto the fathers by the prophets, hath in these last days spoken unto us by His Son, who he hath appointed heir of all things, by whom also he made the worlds…" (Hebrews 1:1-2). This is He in whom you find your rest. The Creator of the heavens and the earth and all that are in them, is also your Redeemer who came to save you from sin and death. If you, by faith, claim Him to be your Creator and accept Him as your Savior and Redeemer, then He simply asks you, "**…Remember the Sabbath day to keep it Holy…**" It is not a burdensome task that He had to do away with. Sabbath keeping is simply a demonstration of our love for the one who created us, saves us and who will ultimately redeem us from a world of sin and woe.

God has encoded this sanctifying principle in His moral law, the Ten Commandments. He simply asks you to keep the Sabbath-day holy as evidence of your trust in Him. The Savior longs to see His character reflected in your life. His desire is for you to uplift Him as your Creator and submit to His will in your life. When, by God's grace, you do just that, you demonstrate to the world your genuine faith in His word. Your obedience to His will is the evidence of your saving relationship with your Creator.

His will is engraved in His law. In the next chapter we will take an insightful look at the Sabbath and the law. We will examine the Sabbath of the Ten Commandments, God's supreme law.

CHAPTER 4
The Sabbath Of The Ten Commandments

The word '**Law**' denotes a legal concept. It is a concept that suggests that someone, in a superior position, puts forth certain rules and regulations, which another, in an inferior position, is bound to follow. If those rules and regulations are violated, then the law provides for certain consequences or punishments. Law is a universal concept. It is the foundation of all human endeavors. All of our affairs in this life are conducted on the basis of law.

In our homes there are laws. The parents lay down the rules and regulations of the home and the children are bound to follow. When the children do contrary to those prescribed rules and regulations, they are sure to meet with the consequences of their disobedience. Perhaps, they will get a spanking or some other form of discipline.

There are rules established by our local governments. For example, we have laws regulating the flow of traffic. If a traffic sign indicates that the speed limit is thirty miles per hour, but you choose to go forty or fifty miles per hour; you are in violation of that law. If caught, you can be made to pay a fine to the city or county government. In some instances, you may even be incarcerated.

Then there are state laws. Your state legislature may pass a law that says residents must register their cars and have them covered by insurance, before you are permitted to drive on the highways and roads. If you fail to abide by those regulations, that law provides for certain penalties, such as fines or revocation of your right to drive.

In the United States of America, as in all other civilized countries, all citizens are obligated to abide by the supreme law of the land called the Constitution. All other laws of the land are subject to that law. The violation thereof can result in serious consequences that may affect anyone in the population.

No rational person would suggest that the laws governing our temporal lives might be broken without suffering the consequences of their violation. Laws and consequences are the foundation of human civilization. It has been that way from creation. It has continued so throughout the history of mankind and will remain thus as long as we exist. Should we do away with, or otherwise eradicate those laws, the result would be chaotic. Violating those laws results in the breakup of the home. Disregarding civil and national laws leads to civil unrest and national catastrophe.

Now, those are only man made laws. It follows, therefore, that the God of the universe must also have laws by which his subjects, mankind, are bound to abide. How much more serious then can be the consequences for the violation of God's laws? The violation of God's law is called sin. The apostle John tells us plainly, "…Whosoever committeth sin transgresseth also the law: for sin Is the transgression of the law…" (1 John 3:4) The consequence for its violation is death. The apostle Paul writes, "..The wages of sin is death…"(Romans 6:23)

All laws have within them a common element called a seal. The seal authenticates the laws that have been laid down. It solidifies and gives validity to the law. It also identifies the lawgiver. The seal always give the sphere of authority to the lawgiver.

In the home, the simple pronouncement from the parent that lets the child know who is in charge constitutes that seal. The parents proclaim who they are…John/Mary (their name) Daddy/Mommy (title) and the territory over which they rule (the home).

Likewise, the local government makes the laws. These laws become effective by affixing the name of the ruling authority, e.g. Michael Bloomberg ,(name), Mayor (title), city of New York (sphere of authority). The law, written on paper, signed by the mayor and affixed with his seal now becomes effective. Anyone who violates it will suffer the consequences.

The same is true of the state. All legislation, in order to become effective, must be signed by the Governor. His seal showing his name, his title and the territory, over which he rules, must be affixed before that legislation becomes law.

So it is with national laws. The national laws of the United States only become effective when signed by the President. His seal affixed thereto showing his name, George W. Bush, his title, President and his territory, the United States of America gives validity and power to the law.

What about God? Does He have a law by which his supreme creation, man, must abide? What are the consequences of violating God's law? Is His law binding upon all men? Do we need to keep it? Does it have a seal? Let us examine the official record to determine what it says.

At creation, God blessed Adam and Eve with everything they needed to enjoy life to its fullest, and to worship Him in completeness. He also laid down some laws. His laws were enshrined in this command, "…The Lord God commanded the man, saying …Of every tree of the garden thou may freely eat; but of the tree of the knowledge of good and evil, thou shall not eat of it, for in the day that thou eat thereof thou shall surely die…." (Genesis 2: 16,17)

God desired man to have the knowledge of good. The apostle James declares: "… Every good gift and every perfect gift is from above, and cometh down from the father of lights, with whom is no variableness, neither shadow of turning..." (James 1:17) But God desires us to avoid and to have no knowledge of evil. The Psalmist David declares, "… Depart from evil, and do good: seek peace, and pursue it…" (Psalms 34:14). This being the case, one may naturally ask, why did God command our first parents not to partake of the tree of the knowledge of good and evil? The answer is a simple one. Good and truth are easily discernable. Evil and lies are also plainly detectable. Man may choose either of these willingly and knowingly. But good mixed with evil is the most dangerous and destructive choice one can ever make. Good mixed with evil is deception. It is the strongest weapon in the arsenal of the devil. This is the lesson God was teaching our first parents. Truth or good by itself will always stand the test of time. Evil and error will fall all the time... But truth mixed with error, or good mixed with evil, will appear to stand but the results are devastating. It is called deception. It is the ace in the arsenal of the adversary.

Unfortunately, this is exactly how our adversary, the devil, approached Eve in Eden. He came to her thus, "... Now, the serpent was more subtle than any beast of the field, which the Lord God had made. And he said unto the woman, 'Yea, hath God said, ye shall not eat of every tree of the garden' (Genesis 3:1) Of course, that was not what God said. The account continues, "... And the woman said unto the serpent... ' We may eat of the trees of the garden; but of the tree which is in the midst of the garden, God hath said, ye shall not eat of it, neither shall ye touch it, lest ye die' (Genesis 3:2,3) To which the serpent assuredly replied: "...Ye shall not surely die, for God know that in the day ye eat thereof, then your eyes shall be opened, and ye shall be as gods, knowing good and evil... "(Genesis 3:4,5). We all know the story. We are experiencing the devastating effects today.

God commanded that she (Eve) should not eat of the tree lest she die and be separated from Him (God). The devil came, in the disguise of a beautiful serpent, misquoted God and led Eve to disobey God's command.

He does the very same thing today with respect to God's law, particularly with regards to the Sabbath commandment. Sadly to say, he has been extremely successful, using the same tactics he used in the Garden of Eden. He continues to mix truth with error. As he deceived Eve, he is deceiving millions today who claim to love God and follow His only begotten son, Jesus Christ. It is quite sad to see so many who profess to love God blatantly disregard His law, particularly the Sabbath commandment. They do this believing they are doing the right thing.

The apostle Paul reaffirmed what God said in the Garden of Eden, "...the wages of sin is death..." (Romans 6:23) And what is sin? It is what Eve did in the Garden of Eden, i.e. disobeying God's law. The apostle John makes it plain: "...Whosoever commits sin, transgress (break) the law; for sin is the transgression of the law..." (1 John 3:4). But which Law? Of all the laws given to man by God, none is of higher value than the Ten Commandments. This law encompasses all other laws and forms the foundation of God's government. It is the supreme law by

which he intends all men to live. It is God's constitution. It reads thus:
(1) Thou shall have no other god before me.
(2) Thou shall not make unto thee any graven image or any likeness of anything that is in heaven above, or that is in the earth beneath, or that is in the water under the earth: thou shall not bow down thyself to them, nor serve them: for I the Lord thy God am a jealous God, visiting the iniquity of the fathers upon the children unto the third and fourth generation of them that hate Me and showing mercy unto thousands of them that love Me and keep my commandments.
(3) Thou shall not take the name of the Lord thy God in vain; for the Lord will not hold him guiltless that take His name in vain.
(4) Remember the Sabbath day to keep it holy. Six days shall thou labor, and do all thy work: but the seventh day is the Sabbath of the Lord thy God: in it thou shall not do any work: thou nor thy son, nor thy daughter, nor thy manservant, nor thy maidservant, nor thy cattle, nor thy stranger that is within thy gates. For in six days The Lord made heaven and earth, the sea and all that in them is, and rested on the seventh day: wherefore the Lord blessed the Sabbath-day and hallowed it.
(5) Honor thy father and thy mother: that thy days may be long upon the land, which the Lord, thy God giveth thee.
(6) Thou shall not kill.
(7) Thou shall not commit adultery.
(8) Thou shall not steal.
(9) Thou shall not bear false witness against thy neighbor.
(10) Thou shall not covet thy neighbor's house. Thou shall not covet thy neighbor's wife: nor his manservant, nor his maidservant, nor his ox, nor his ass, nor anything that is thy neighbor's. (Exodus 20:3-17)

The questions now to be answered, by those who claim that

God's Law has been done away with, are, 'which of God's laws have been done away with... and when did God do away with it?' Which one, I ask, don't we have to abide by when we become Christians thus accepting Jesus Christ as our Lord and Savior?

The apostle Paul reminds us, "...Because the law worketh wrath: for where no law is, there is no transgression...." (Romans 4:15) He continues, "...Wherefore the law is holy, and the commandment holy, and just, and good..." (Romans 7:12)

Of this law, Jesus, when confronted by a lawyer, who asked Him,"... Master, what is the great commandment in the law...", declared, "...Thou shalt love the Lord thy God with all thy heart, and with all thy soul, and with all thy mind. This is the first and great commandment. And the second is like unto it, thou shalt love thy neighbor as thy self. On these two commandments hang all the law and the prophets..." (Matthew 22: 37-40)

What Jesus in effect did was to give a summary of the Ten Commandments. He further declared them to be the foundation of God's government. Verses 37 and 38 tell us how we should love, honor and worship God. We do so by obeying the first four commandments. (See Ten Commandments previously quoted) Verse 39 teaches us how we are to love and relate to our fellow men. We do so by obeying the last six commandments.

The learned apostle Paul, agrees with his Savior. He writes to the saints in Rome, "...Love worketh no ill to his neighbor; therefore love is the fulfilling of the law..." (Romans 13:10)

How can men misunderstand so simple a principle, is beyond the understanding of this writer. Man's smartness mixed with God's truth produces intellectual darkness. Such is the manifestation of the teaching of God's law being abandoned.

If any of God's laws have been done away with, then all of them must also be done away with. James, the Lord's brother, writes, "...For whosoever shall keep the whole law, and yet offend in one point, he is guilty of all..." (James 2:10)

I thank God that nowhere in His word do we find Him annulling any part of his law.

Not unlike the man-made laws we discussed earlier, when we carefully examine God's supreme law, His Ten Commandments, we find His seal affixed thereto. The Sabbath commandment is that seal. In it we find the name of the lawgiver- The Lord thy God. His title is also revealed -The Creator. His territory is likewise explicitly stated - the heaven, the earth, the sea and all that in them is (Exodus 20:8-11).

Of all the precepts of God's law, the Sabbath commandment is the only one that He admonishes us in a positive, emphatic way to remember. God says,"…Remember the Sabbath day to keep it Holy…" (Exodus 20:8).

God knew well the dark shadow that would be cast upon His law by the great deceiver.

Remaining true to his methods and mode of operation in Eden, the devil continues to cast doubt and reproach upon God's law. He continues to mix truth with error in deceiving men to trample upon God's Sabbath. Unfortunately, men continue to eat of the fruit of knowledge of good and evil and are thus deceived. With regards to the law and the Sabbath, Satan beguiles men by leading them to proclaim that we are no longer under law but under grace.

Their minds have become darkened with this deceptive sophistry that appeals to man's carnal nature. Like in Eden, the devil causes his disciples, who appear as ministers of light, to use God's word to advance his, (Satan's), lies. The great deceiver is leading untold millions, through his chosen vessels, to their eternal deaths.

The favorite past time, for those who preach the devil's lies, is to misquote the apostle Paul. They cite, "…For sin shall not have dominion over you: for ye are not under the law, but under grace…" (Romans 6:14). They completely avoid the very next Scripture which says, "…what then? Shall we sin (break the law) because we are not under the law, but under grace? God forbid…" (Romans 6:15).

Paul asks the same question again, "…what shall we say then? Shall we continue in sin (continue to break the law), that grace may abound? (Romans 6:1). He makes it even plainer, "…Do we then make void the law of God through faith? God forbid, yea, we establish the law… " (Romans 3:31).

The law to which Paul is referring in each of these cases is the Ten Commandment law with its seal, the Sabbath commandment. Jesus established that fact by declaring the Ten Commandments to be the constitution of God's government. (Matthew 22:37-40, *quoted earlier*)

A correct understanding of what grace is, and how Paul relates it to the law is necessary for properly comprehending what Paul is talking about. Here is an explanation. Biblical grace is a divine endowment. It is bestowed freely and abundantly to every man from God. Grace affords us pardon from our sins. Grace further empowers us to live without sin. Grace saves us from the condemnation of sin, which is death. Grace is that which God gives to us that we may have a chance to return to Him. It is not, like so many teach, a license to break God's law. Indeed it is the power to keep us from breaking the law, which is sin. It is a free gift given by a Holy God to undeserving man. Grace is the divine influence upon the heart, drawing sinful man ever closer to his Holy Creator.

Jesus declared to the woman, caught in adultery, who was about to suffer the consequences of her sin, "…Neither do I condemn thee: go and sin no more …" (John 8:11).
This is the epitome of grace. Amazing grace, marvelous grace. Notice, Jesus did not tell the woman to go and commit more adultery because of His grace towards her. He forgave and then empowered her to sin no more. To not sin, means to keep the law. If the law is no longer in existence, then how can we sin no more?

So, when Paul declares that we are not under the law, but under grace; he is simply saying that we have been pardoned by a merciful God, through the atoning sacrifice of Jesus Christ, from the condemnation of the law, which is death.

Paul concludes, "… but the gift of God is eternal life through Christ Jesus…" (Romans 6:23)

That is the miracle of the Gospel. It is the power that leads us to keep the law, through the indwelling of Jesus in our hearts. We cannot separate the law from the Gospel. They are indivisible halves of the same whole.

Clearly, Paul is not giving permission to sin because of God's grace to us through Our Lord and Savior Jesus Christ. Rather, he is calling the Christian to a higher standard of accountability. He is pointing us to keep the law by the grace of God, because of our love for Him.

As Christians, our determination should be not to sin, i.e. breaking any of God's commandments. Because of our human nature, we do, from time to time, fall into temptation and sin. Thanks to God for grace. Because of that grace so freely and abundantly given to us, our lives should reflect the character of God. His character is exemplified by His Holy Law, the Ten Commandments. Those commandments include the command to keep the Sabbath day holy.

The apostle John presents true grace to us. He counsels, "…My little children, these things write I unto you, that ye sin not. And if any man sin, we have an advocate with the Father, Jesus Christ the righteous. And He is the propitiation for our sins: and not for our sins only, but also for the sins of the whole world…" (1 John 2: 1,2)

Being saved by grace means the turning away from sin and walking in righteousness. It lovingly demands the end of breaking God's law and the beginning of obeying it. We can obey only by the power of the indwelling of the Holy Spirit coupled with a willing and submissive heart.

Since sin is the breaking of God's law, then salvation must be the return to keeping God's law. The angel declared to Joseph, "…And she shall bring forth a son and thou shall call His name JESUS; for He shall save His people from their sin… (Matthew 1:21)

Jesus did not die the ignominious death He died so that we should not continue in sin. He certainly did not leave the glory of heaven and come to this sinful world to save us in our sins. His mission is to eradicate sin completely from our lives. It is His purpose to restore us to that Edenic image, which is a life without sin. A life without sin means a life that is in total obedience to the commandments of God, His Sabbath commandment includeed.

Consider this for a moment. If there is no law, then there must be no sin. For sin is the transgression of the law. (1 John 3:4). If there is no sin then we have no need of a Savior. Since there is no need for a Savior, then we don't need the Gospel. Now that we have no need of the

Gospel, we certainly have no purpose for a preacher to preach the Gospel and to teach the Bible, which is the Gospel. Perhaps the next time a so called preacher tells you that God's law is abolished, you can ask him or her why are they preaching and what are they teaching.

As we consider Jesus and His relationship to the law, we will discover that He kept the whole law perfectly. Paul declares, "...For we have not an high priest which cannot be touched with the feeling of our infirmities: but was in all points tempted like as we are, yet without sin..." (Hebrews 4:15). Jesus is not only our sinless High Priest, but he is also our example. Peter writes, "...For even hereunto were ye called: because Christ also suffered for us, leaving us an example that we should follow his steps..." (1Peter 2:21).

If Jesus is our example, and He is; and if He kept the law perfectly, and He did; then we also must, by His grace, keep the law. That law includes the Sabbath commandment that says, "...Remember the Sabbath day to keep it holy..." (Exodus 20:8)
Jesus further declares: "...If ye love me, keep my commandments..." (John 14:15)

The apostle John makes it plain: "...By this we know that we love the children of God, when we love God and keep his commandments...For this is the love of God that we keep his commandments: and His commandments are not grievous..." (1 John 5:2,3).

Neither Paul, nor John nor our Lord and Savior Jesus Christ were addressing the Jews of the Old Testament exclusively when these statements were made. They were confirming what God had ordained and taught through his prophets, before them. They were speaking to the New Testament believers, both Jews and Gentiles alike. These are those who accept Jesus Christ as their personal Savior from sin and death.

The law Jesus and the apostles were all referring to, was the Ten Commandment law with its seal, the Sabbath commandment, which admonishes us, "...Remember the Sabbath day to keep it holy. Six days shall thou labor, and do all thy work: but the seventh day is the Sabbath of the Lord thy God, in it thou shall not do any work, thou nor thy son, nor thy daughter, thy manservant, nor thy maidservant, nor thy cattle, nor thy stranger that is within thy gates: For in six days the Lord made the heaven and earth, the sea and all that in them is, and rested on the seventh day: Wherefore the Lord blessed the Sabbath-day, and hallowed it." (Exodus 20: 8-11)

God's moral law, including His Sabbath commandment, was not just for the Jews of old. It is for all men in all times. The psalmist David recognized this. He declared, "...The works of His hands are verity and judgment; all his commandments are sure.... they stand fast forever and ever, and are done in truth and uprightness… "(Psalm 111:7-8) David continued, "…Thy righteousness is an everlasting righteousness, and thy law is truth…" (Psalm 119: 142).

What is your standard of righteousness if it is not the law of God? Ponder that thought for a moment. Declaring the moral law of God annulled because of Jesus' sacrifice on Calvary is to eat of the fruit of the knowledge of good and evil. It is a deception of the devil. As God's people, we must not only avoid such a teaching, we must vigorously oppose it. Anyone who teaches such is not echoing the voice of God or teaching the word of God. The prophet Isaiah admonishes us, "…To the law and the testimony: if they speak not according to this word, it is because there is no light in them..." (Isaiah 8:20). No light means there is darkness. Such teaching is not the work of light, but of darkness. The apostle John puts it even more forcibly, "…And hereby we know that we know Him if we keep His commandments... he that says I know him and keep not his commandments, is a liar, and the truth is not in him…" (1John 2:3,4).

Our Lord and Savior emphatically declared: "…Think not that I am come to destroy the law, or the prophets. I am not come to destroy, but to fulfill. For verily I say unto you, till heaven and earth pass, one jot or one tittle shall in no wise pass from the law, till all be fulfilled. Whosoever therefore break one of these least commandments, and shall teach men so, he shall be called the least in heaven: but whosoever shall do and teach them, the same shall be called great in the kingdom of heaven…" (Matthew 5:17-19)

Jesus' fulfillment of the law was prophesied by the prophet Isaiah thus, "…The Lord is well pleased for His righteousness' sake: He will magnify the law and make it honorable..." (Isaiah 42:21)

His fulfillment of the law is not to do away with it; but rather to make it more clear through His living example. He kept it perfectly as an example for us to follow. Jesus never asks us what we think about the law, or what does Paul say about it. He simply beckons us to follow Him. John again declares, "... He that says he abides in Him ought himself also to walk, even as he (Jesus) walked..." (1 John 2:6). And how did Jesus walk in reference to the law. The Savior declares,"...If ye keep My commandments, ye shall abide in My love; even as I have kept my Father's commandments, and abide in His love..." (John 15:10)

Jesus never worshiped any other God besides His Father. Neither should we. He kept the Sabbath-day holy and so should we. He never disrespected his parents and we should not either. He never committed adultery. He never stole. He never lied. He never killed anyone. He never coveted anything that was not His. Anyone who professes to follow Him must do likewise. His mission and His desire are to empower us to keep His law so that we will be fit for heaven where there is no sin (law-breaking).

Jesus came to this earth to save us from our sins, and not in our sins. To put it another way: Jesus, by His grace, will empower us to keep His law. His coming to earth does not give us a license to trample upon His law. Sin, as is already pointed out, is the breaking of God's law. His holy moral law is His Ten Commandments. It includes the Sabbath commandment enjoining all His people to keep it holy. The Sabbath commandment is God's sign to us that He is the true God, the One that created us. Thus, from creation, God blessed the Sabbath day and made it holy. All He asks us to do is to remember to keep it holy.

Before we subscribe to the satanic teaching and impure notion that God's law, including its seal, His Sabbath commandment, is done away with; consider this. What would be the result if you did away with the laws of your home? What would happen if the laws of your city or state were abandoned? What would happen if the constitution of your country was discarded?

Though these laws exist, we see the consequences of men not obeying them. Crime, violence, lasciviousness, pain, suffering and death

permeate our society. Imagine then if these laws were suddenly cancelled. You cannot conceive with the heart or commit by pen what would be the result of such
actions.

Now, try to picture the God of Heaven abandoning His law, the Ten Commandments. The result would be frightening and unimaginable.

False prophets of this deadly heresy are not speaking for God. They are not teaching according to the law and the testimony. Certainly they are not following the example of our Lord and Savior Jesus Christ. Since all have sinned (broken God's law) and come short of the glory of God; then in order to be restored to his glory, we must return to keeping His law.

This is the purpose for which Jesus came, died and lives. That we may be restored to our Edenic image is God's ideal for us. It is higher than our highest thoughts of ourselves.

To teach that we do not have to keep His law, yet would be restored to God's image, is perpetuating the original lie of the devil, "... Ye shall not surely die. For God doth know that in the day ye eat thereof (disobey God/ cast aside His commandment), then your eyes will be opened, and ye shall be as gods, knowing good and evil... "(Genesis 3:5-6). To believe and teach such is partaking of the fruit of the tree of good and evil. It was a lie in Eden and it is a lie today.

Jesus Christ, our Creator, Savior, Redeemer and Lawgiver, is the only example we should follow. He kept the law including the Sabbath commandment and we must too.

As the world (including many preachers and teachers who previously had proclaimed that God's law was abandoned by His grace) is now calling attention to the Ten Commandments, you would be wise to ask them if the Sabbath commandment is included in the Ten they are promoting. This would lead to interesting conversation.

But who has attempted to change God's law and who is leading men to dishonor the God of creation? Who is it that seeks our worship and teaches us to trample upon God's holy Sabbath? This we will discover in our next chapter, From Sabbath to Sunday.

CHAPTER 5

From Sabbath To Sunday

We have traced the consistency of God's Sabbath from creation to Jesus. We have discovered its immovable status in God's law. Let's now examine how and by whom the attempted change from Sabbath to Sunday has come about. You will find that the evidence is irrefutable and the record clear.

We are involved in a great controversy. It is a battle that began in heaven and is raging on earth. John the Revelator tells us,"...And there was war in heaven: Michael and His angels fought against the dragon; and the dragon fought against his angels...and prevailed not; neither was their place found no more in heaven, and the great dragon was cast out, and that old serpent, called the devil and Satan which deceives the whole world: he was cast out into the earth, and his angels were cast out with him..." (Revelation 12: 7-9).

This conflict is a battle for our minds and our worship. It is a battle of cosmic proportions involving Christ and Satan. We are the pawns and prizes of this conflict, depending on whose side we choose. For every true Bible doctrine given to us by God, the devil has a counterfeit. The seventh-day Sabbath is the truth. Sunday sacredness is the counterfeit.

The good news is that Christ has already won the battle. His earnest desire is that we will be His witness to this fact. If we choose Him and follow His ways, then we become His trophies. We can only be those trophies of Jesus and witnesses for Him if our religion is based not on the traditions and customs of men, pronouncements of the learned and educated, or the decrees of ecclesiastical councils; but purely and solely on the word of God. Only those who have fortified their minds with the truths of the Bible will be trophies for Jesus.

The word of God does not in any way annul, abrogate or

otherwise disavow the Sabbath-day. As we have shown thus far, God established the Sabbath-day at creation and gave it to all mankind as a gift. The prophets preached it and reminded God's people of its sacredness. Jesus kept it and taught His disciples to do likewise. The apostles remained faithful to the Sabbath throughout their ministries. God incorporated it into his holy moral code, the Ten Commandments. It is for the benefit of all mankind in all ages.

Of such importance is the Sabbath day to God that He made its observance the emblem of man's sanctification and evidence of their true loyalty to Him. Moses says to the people of Israel, "…wherefore the children of Israel shall keep the Sabbath throughout their generations, for a perpetual covenant, it is a sign between me and the children of Israel forever: for in six days the Lord made heaven and earth, and on the seventh day He rested, and was refreshed …" (Exodus 31:16,17)

We have found out that as Christians, we are all Israel and the Sabbath is therefore for us also. Paul teaches, "…and if ye be Christ's, then are ye Abraham's seed, and heirs according to the promise…" (Galatians 3:29)

But why do men claim that the Sabbath was not only changed, but that another day was substituted in its place? Where did that doctrine originate? The proof of such attempted change will be presented in this chapter.

The prophet Isaiah, in describing the mind of our great adversary, satan, declared thus, "…How art thou fallen from heaven, O Lucifer, son of the morning: how art thou cut down to the ground, which didst weaken the nations… For thou hast said in thine heart, I will ascend into heaven, I will exalt my throne above the stars of God: I will sit also upon the mount of the congregation, in the sides of the north… I will ascend about the heights of the clouds: I will be like the Most High. Yet thou shall be brought down to hell, to the sides of the pit. They that see thee shall narrowly look upon, and consider thee, saying "… Is this the man that made the earth to tremble that did shake the kingdoms…" (Isaiah 14:12-16)

In thus enunciating the heart and intentions of satan, (Lucifer, before he was cast out of heaven), the prophet Isaiah was allegorically describing the kingdom of Babylon and its ruler, Nebuchadnezzar. The prophet is talking about that spirit of rebellion which seeks to rise itself above God and usurp His authority as ruler of the universe. It is the spirit of antichrist.

Paul likewise, in speaking of that king and kingdom that would in the end of time manifest the spirit of satan in seeking to overthrow God and usurp His authority in men's hearts, declared, "...Let no man deceive you by any means: for that day shall not come, except there come a falling away first, and that man of sin be revealed, the son of perdition; who opposes and exalts himself above all that is called God, or that is worshipped; so that he as God sits in the temple of God, showing that he is God...." (2 Thessalonians 2:3-4)

Paul's account of that antichrist spirit is remarkably similar to that of Isaiah's as recorded in Isaiah 14: 12 -16. He, the one who opposes God, is satan. He was once part of God's family. Satan presumes that he can take the place of God and obtain the worship of God's people. This spirit of usurpation was manifested not only in the king of Babylon of old; but the apostle John predicts that the same spirit will be manifested in an entity at the end of time which he (John), under the inspiration of God, calls, "...Mystery Babylon the great, the mother of harlots and abominations of the earth..." (Revelation 17: 5)

What more effective way is there to attempt to usurp the throne of the God of the universe than by attacking his law and proposing to change it? And, what greater effect would that attack have than to seek to remove God's seal (His Blessed Sabbath day) and replace it with its (Mystery Babylon) mark of authority?

This is exactly what the prophet Daniel predicted the antichrist power will do. He prophesied, "...And he (antichrist) will speak great words against the Most High, and shall wear out the saints of the Most High and "THINK" to change times and laws..." (Daniel 7:25)

The only one of God's Ten Commandments that deals with time is the Sabbath commandment. (Exodus 20: 8 -11) As already pointed out in previous chapters, observance of the seventh-day Sabbath is evidence of one's true obedience and submission to the God of creation. But what does satan want to accomplish? He desires and works untiringly and deceptively to obtain the worship of man, which only the God of creation deserves.

So, what does the great deceiver do? He works through his chosen instrumentalities, men and organizations, to establish a false day of worship. He institutes and promotes to the world a day branded with his mark of authority.

The devil has done a phenomenal job in accomplishing this goal though his chosen agencies. Paul proclaims, "... For such are false apostles, deceitful workers, transforming themselves into the apostles of Christ: And no marvel; for satan himself is transformed into an angel of light...therefore it is no great thing if his ministers also be transformed as the ministers of righteousness; whose end shall be according to their works..." (2 Corinthians 11: 13-15)

The apostle Peter likewise concludes, "...But there were false prophets (those who do not speak according to the law and the testimony) also among the people, even as there shall be false teachers among you, who privily shall bring in damnable heresies, even denying the Lord that brought them, and bring upon themselves swift destruction...And many shall follow their pernicious ways; by reason of whom the way of truth shall evil be spoken of...And through covetousness shall they with feigned words make merchandise of you; whose judgment now of a long time lingers not, and their damnation slumbers not... which have forsaken the right way, and are gone astray, following the way of Balaam, the son of Bosor, who loved the wages of unrighteousness...These are wells without water, clouds that are carried with a tempest; to whom the mist of darkness is forever..." (2 Peter 2: 1-3,15-17).

Such are the preachers and teachers who proclaim that God has changed his Sabbath-day from the seventh day of the week to the first. The Scripture, of course, reveals no such change on God's part. Neither God, nor Jesus, nor the apostles taught such a doctrine. The Scripture does, however, clearly point out that man will attempt to make that change.

The pagan religions of old worshipped many so-called gods. There were gods for different seasons of the year. There were gods for the several elements of nature. Every aspect of their religion revolved around the worship of a specific god so-called for a specific purpose. All of those religions, of which the Babylonian mystery religion was the foundation, venerated the sun as their main God. They attached great significance to the sun, as a source of all life. It was revered for its life giving powers. The sun-worshippers, therefore, dedicated the first day of the week, today called Sunday, to the sun. They worshipped the sun as their chief god.

This practice was pervasive. So much so that God's people, in apostasy, were engulfed with it. The prophet Ezekiel reports, "... Then said He unto me, hast thou seen this, O son of man? Turn thee yet again, and thou shall see greater abominations than these...and He brought me into the inner court of the Lord's house, and behold, at the door of the temple of the Lord, between the porch and the altar, were about five and twenty men, with their backs toward the temple of the Lord, and their faces toward the east; and they worshipped the sun toward the east..." (Ezekiel 8:15-16). Shortly after this revelation to Ezekiel, God sent swift destruction upon Israel. (See Ezekiel Chapter 9)

God calls Sunday sacredness an abomination. It is idolatry of the highest order. It is a tradition of men and not a commandment of God. God abhors this pagan practice of worshipping the sun. Rather, God desires us to worship Him, the God who created the sun. Jesus asks, "... Why call me Lord, Lord and do not the things that I say..." (Luke 6:46) What He says is that the Sabbath-day is the seventh day of the week, today called Saturday; not Sunday, which is the first day.

Sun worship is a practice that has been prevalent throughout the history of man. It can be traced as far back to the time of Nimrod. (Genesis Chapter 10). After his death, his wife Sereramis, believing that he had ascended to the sun, instituted the worship of the sun in recognition of Nimrod as a god. This practice spread throughout the then known world. It has found a place in every culture known to man.

Sun worship was deeply endeared by pagan religions during early apostolic times. It was practiced by the many false religions against which the apostles preached.

The true Gospel, as practiced and taught by the early Christians, proved severely problematic to their imperial rulers, the Caesars of Rome who were all sun worshippers. The true Gospel taught men and women to keep the Sabbath-day (the seventh day of the week) holy. It is a Gospel that does not teach Sunday sacredness or endorses venerating the sun.

The apostle Paul records that the true Gospel, preached with such fervency and accompanied by the power of the Holy Spirit, had reached the house of the Caesars. He records in his letter to the Philippians from his abode in Rome, "…All the saints salute you, chiefly they that are of Caesar's household.…" (Philippians 4:22)

The fires of persecution, set ablaze against the Christians by the sun-worshipping, Sunday-keeping pagans, served as the fuel that propelled the true Gospel throughout the Roman Empire. Severe persecution did not, as the Romans hoped, obliterate the religion of Christ. Despite the relentless persecutions of Nero, Diocletian and other Roman emperors; the pure, unadulterated Gospel of Jesus Christ continued to reach men's hearts. The message of salvation through Jesus Christ alone turned many away from their pagan traditions, centered in sun worship.

Men and women were led to a risen Savior and His charge to obey the laws of God. Penitent souls were pointed to a sin pardoning, loving Savior who called them to his rest, and to obey his commandments, the Sabbath commandment included. This constituted a major problem for the sun worshipping Caesars and their followers. Persecution of the true Christians did not solve the problem of the Caesars. Instead, it advanced the cause of Jesus Christ. In the face of unrelenting persecution, the early Christian church grew rapidly throughout the Roman Empire.

And then came Constantine. As Roman emperor in the early 4th century, he recognized, quite unlike his predecessors, that persecution of the Christians was not helping at all to strengthen the empire or to advance his purposes. He realized that persecution of the growing Christian church was not the answer to the empire's problems. He chose, therefore, to adopt the policy of ' If you can't beat them join them.'

Constantine, not unlike his contemporaries, was an avowed

sun worshiper. He exalted and paid homage to the Persian sun deity, Mithra. Mithraism was but one of the many pagan religions practiced throughout the empire. Like all of those pagan religions, Mithraism was centered in sun worship and accorded highest honors to the first day of the week, today called Sunday.

Some Christians, in an effort to separate themselves from the Jews, whom they thought of as evil because of their (the Jews) crucifixion of Jesus Christ, also began to venerate the first day of the week. By so doing, they thought they were distinguishing themselves from the wicked Jews. It seemed a good thing to do. They found great comfort in the idea that they were honoring Jesus by commemorating His resurrection.

Historian E.M. Chalmers writes, "…These Gentile Christians of Rome and Alexandria began calling the first day of the week the Lord's Day. This was not difficult for the pagans of the Roman Empire who were steeped in sun worship to accept, because they (the pagans) referred to their sun god as their Lord…" (**How Sunday came into the Christian Church,** page 3)

The Scripture does say that Jesus rose from the dead on the first day of the week. (Matthew 28: 1-6) However, there is no command in all of Scripture that enjoins men to keep Sunday holy. Such a practice is, as we are discovering, a tradition of men.

God did not make the first day holy. Since the God of creation is the only One who can make anything holy, Sunday can never be a holy day. The day God made holy is the seventh-day, today called Saturday; not the first, which is called Sunday. (Genesis 2:2,3). No man therefore can make the first day, or any other day holy.

Like any astute politician who seeks the support of his people and wishes to consolidate his power, Constantine came up with a brilliant idea. He seized the opportunity and took advantage of the situation to strengthen his own position as emperor and to bolster an already failing empire.

He professed to accept the religion of the Christians. He further decreed that the first day of the week, Sunday, will become the official day of worship throughout the empire. Later, it was reported that

Constantine had a vision, at noontime, whilst on one of his military campaigns. In the vision, Constantine was reported to have seen a massive cross above the sun (which he worshipped as god). The cross was purportedly adorned with the inscription "Conquer by this". Hence the sight of crosses all around us, supposedly uplifting our Lord and Savior Jesus Christ.

This marked the official beginning of the practice of Sunday sacredness in the Christian church. By Constantine's supposed conversion, a plethora of pagan practices were established in the early church. Two of the most prominent were: firstly, Sunday sacredness and, secondly, image worship. Many other practices, such as mother/son worship, praying the rosary, baby baptisms, prayers for the dead, adoration of icons and saints, and such like, were also adopted into the Christian faith.

With Constantine's supposed conversion, the amalgamation of corrupt pagan practices with the pure religion of Jesus Christ was established. Not only were the religions of paganism and Christianity joined together; but also the state was joined to the now corrupt faith. Constantine, as head of the Roman state, also became head of the newly amalgamated religion. He took upon himself the title of Pontifex Maximus, supreme pontiff.

Thus, Constantine, by definition, became the first pope of Rome. This title, along with the many other pagan practices, were adapted directly or indirectly from the ancient mystery religion of Babylon.

As a result of these and other similar actions, the true Christian faith started on its downward slide into apostasy. The historian William D. Kileen writes in his book, **The Ancient Church**, page 26, "…Rites and ceremonies, of which Paul nor Peter never heard, crept silently into use, and then claimed the rank of divine institutions. Church officers for whom the primitive disciples could have found no place, and titles which to them would have been altogether unintelligible, began to challenge attention and to be named apostolic…"

Such were the effects of Constantine's purported conversion to the Christian faith. It brought in the lies and deceit of the devil and mingled them with the truth and holiness of God. Constantine planted the seed of the tree of knowledge of good and evil. That tree has grown and blossomed its fruit of almost universal apostasy through the acceptance of Sunday in the place of God's true Sabbath. He mixed error with truth, the deadliest of all deceptions.

Constantine's rest day (Sunday) decree reads thus,"… On the venerable day of the sun (the sacred day) let the magistrates and people residing in the cities rest, and let all the workshops be closed. In the country, however, persons engaged in agriculture may freely and lawfully continue their pursuits; because it often happens that another day is not suitable for grain sowing or for vine planting; lest by neglecting the proper moment for such operations the bounty of heaven should be lost- Given the 7th day of March AD 321. (**Codex Justinianus-The first Sunday Law of Constantine I**). This decree was progressively strengthened by later decrees passed in subsequent church councils in 343AD, 538AD, 578AD and onward.

Noted historian Arthur Weigall similarly confirmed this in his book, **The Paganism in Our Christianity**. He writes on page 145,"… The church (Rome) made a sacred day of Sunday… largely because it was the weekly festival of the sun; for it was a definite Christian policy to take over the pagan festivals endeared to the people by tradition and give them Christian significance…"

Another historian writes of this apostasy,"…Remains of the struggle between the religion of Christianity and the religion of Mithraism are found in two institutions adopted from its rival by Christianity in the fourth century, the two Mithraic sacred days: December 25 dies natalis solis" (birthday of the sun) as the birthday of Jesus; and Sunday, the venerable day of the sun, as Constantine called it in his edict of 321 AD…" (**Paganism to Christianity in the Roman Empire, page** 60, Walter Woodburn Hyde).

Neither the God of creation and of the Sabbath, nor his holy prophets, and most assuredly, not Jesus, endorsed such a change from the seventh-day Sabbath to the first day of the week, Sunday.

Augustus Neander in his classic, **The History of the Christian Religion And The Church,** confirms on page 186, "… The festival of Sunday, like all other festivals was always only a human ordinance and it was far from the intentions of the apostles to establish a Divine command in this respect, far from them, and from the early apostolic church, to transfer the laws of the Sabbath to Sunday…"

Sunday sacredness is the religion of satan. Anyone who teaches or observes it, knowingly or unknowingly, is worshipping, not the God of Heaven, but the great deceiver, satan, who inspired it. There is, however, still hope in Jesus Christ. Paul writes, "…For God commanded His love towards us, for while we were yet sinners Christ died for us…" (Romans 5:8). Trampling on God's Holy Sabbath-day and uplifting Sunday is sin. But God offers a way of escape. Luke concurs, "… And the times of this ignorance God winked at, but now commands all men everywhere to repent…" (Acts 17:30).

If you have read this book to this point, then understanding the Sabbath of the Ten Commandments ought to be clearer to you. If you have hitherto thought that Sunday sacredness is of God, and have been deceived into honoring it, under whatever pretext, then it is time that you repent. Let go and let God. Do not allow satan to hold sway over you and rule your life. Paul admonishes us, "…know ye not, that to whom ye yield yourselves servants to obey, his servants ye are to whom ye obey; whether of sin unto death or of obedience unto righteousness?" (Romans 6:16)

Sunday sacredness is the modern manifestation of sun worship. Attempting to keep Sunday holy is not worshipping God, but rather dishonoring Him. It is dishonoring Him by worshipping the creature instead of the creator.

Who are you obeying on the matter of the Sabbath? God your creator, who gave it to you as a special gift to remind you of who He is; or a man, the pope of Rome, who claims to be God and has the power to change God's law? **THINK ABOUT IT.**

God's Sabbath–day is the seventh day of the week, today called Saturday. (Exodus 20:8-11) Sunday is the first day. Don't be deceived into falling into the devil's trap. His only objective is to rob and destroy God's people. Sunday sacredness is one of his most effective weapons. No man or organization can undo what the God of creation has done. He has established the seventh-day as a memorial of His creative power. The devil seeks to establish Sunday as his mark of authority in men's lives.

The historians continue to reveal the source of the attempted change. "...Is it not strange that Sunday is about universally observed when the sacred writings do not endorse it? Satan, the great counterfeiter worked through the mystery of iniquity to introduce a counterfeit sabbath to take the place of the true Sabbath. Sunday stands side by side with Ash Wednesday, Palm Sunday, Holy Thursday, Good Friday, Easter Sunday, Whitsunday, Corpus Christi, Assumption Day, All Souls day (Halloween), Christmas day and a host of other ecclesiastical feast days too numerous to mention. This array of Roman Catholic feast and fast days are all man made. None of them bear the Divine credentials of the Author of the inspired Word..." **(Historian M. E. Walsh)**

Again we read, "...Sun worship was the earliest idolatry..." **(Fausset Bible Dictionary, page 666)**. "...*Sun worship was one of the oldest of components of the Roman religion...* "**(The Cult of Sol Invictus – The Invincible Sun, page 26, Gaston H. Halsberge)**

The pagan custom of sun worship, having been amalgamated into the Christian religion, provided the basis for the universal state church. As the pagan Roman Empire disintegrated, it gave way to the now apostate religious entity called the Roman Catholic Church. Imperial Rome, having lost its political and military strength, turned to the ever growing and influential church to provide the glue needed to hold the empire together. The church, steeped in paganism but professing to be Christian, willingly provided the cohesion for the empire, which was rapidly slipping away from the grip of the Caesars. That cohesive glue was religion. Not the true religion of Christ; but paganism in the name of Christianity.

The year 538AD was a significant one in the history of the Roman Empire. This was the year in which Emperor Justinian's general, Belasarius, under the authority and protection of the pope of Rome, captured and eradicated the Ostrogoths from the city of Rome and the history books.

The Ostrogoths were the last of the Arian resisters who opposed the church's rule. With their eradication, the church now consolidated its grip on political power and moved into full control of the empire. Pagan Rome had now given way to Papal Rome.

Historian H.G. Guinness sums it up thus,"…The power of the Caesars lived again in the universal dominion of the popes. (**Romanism and the Reformation**).

The practice of Sunday sacredness, which is in effect sun worship, grew to become the mark of authority of the Roman Catholic church. The following statements are evidences of that fact. They are also proof positive of the Roman Catholic church's attempted change from Sabbath to Sunday. They illustrate the significance that the Roman Catholic church attaches to that alleged change. These statements are the manifestation of that spirit of antichrist which the apostle Paul and the prophets Daniel and Isaiah referred to.

Here is what that organization, also referred to as the Papacy, says about the attempted change from the Lord's Sabbath, the seventh day, to Sunday, the first day, the day of the sun. Sunday keeping Christians need to pay close attention.

"…Sunday is a Catholic Institution, and its claims to observance can be defended only on Catholic principles…From beginning to end of Scripture there is not a single passage that warrants the transfer of weekly public worship from the last day of the week to the first…" (**The Catholic Press**, Sydney, Australia, August 1900).

"…Protestantism, in discarding the authority of the (Roman Catholic) Church, has no good reasons for its Sunday theory, and ought logically to keep Saturday as the Sabbath…" (John Gilmar Shea, **American Catholic Quarterly Review**, January 1883.)

"…It is well to remind the Presbyterians, Baptists, Methodists, and all other Christians, that the Bible does not support them anywhere in their observance of Sunday. Sunday is an institution of the Roman Catholic Church, and those who observe the day observe a commandment of the Catholic Church…" (Priest Brady, in an address reported in the **Elizabeth, N.J. News**, March 18, 1903.)

Question: "… Have you any other way of proving that the (Catholic) Church has power to institute festivals or precepts (to command holy days)?"

Answer: "... Had she not such power, she could not have done that in which all modern religionists agree with her: She could not have substituted the observance of Sunday the first day of the week, for the observance of Saturday the seventh day, a change for which there is no Scriptural authority ..." (Stephen Keenan, **A Doctrinal Catechism**, page 176.)

"...Reason and common sense demand the acceptance of one or the other of these alternatives: either Protestantism and the keeping holy of Saturday, or Catholicity and the keeping holy of Sunday. Compromise is impossible..." (**The Catholic Mirror**, December 23, 1893.)

"...God simply gave His (Catholic) Church the power to set aside whatever day or days, she would deem suitable as holy days. The Church chose Sunday, the first day of the week, and the course of time added other days, as holy days..." (Vincent J. Kelly, **Forbidden Sunday and Feast-day Occupations**, page 2.) Of course, God never gave any man or organization that authority.

"...Protestants accept Sunday rather than Saturday as the day for public worship after the Catholic Church made the change...but, the Protestant mind does not seem to realize that, in observing the Sunday, they are accepting the authority of the spokesman for the church, the pope..." (**Our Sunday Visitor**, February 5, 1950.)

"...Not the Creator of the Universe, in Genesis 2:1-3, - but the Catholic Church can claim the honor of having granted man a pause to his work every seven days...." (S.D. Mosna, **Storia della Domenica**, 1969, pages 366-367.)

"...If Protestants would follow the Bible, they should worship God on the Sabbath-day. In keeping the Sunday, they are following a law of the Catholic Church..." (**Albert Smith, Chancellor of the Archdiocese of Baltimore**, replying for the Cardinal, in a letter, February 10, 1920)

"...It was the Catholic Church which, by the authority of Jesus Christ, has transferred this rest (from the Bible Sabbath) to the Sunday. Thus the observance of Sunday by the Protestants is an homage they pay, in spite of themselves, to the authority of the (Catholic) Church..." (Monsignor Louis Segur, **Plain Talk about the Protestantism of Today**, page 213.)

"...We observe Sunday instead of Saturday because the Catholic Church transferred the solemnity from Saturday to Sunday..." (Peter Geiermann, CSSR, **A Doctrinal Catechism**, 1957 edition, page 50)

"...We Catholics, then, have precisely the same authority for keeping Sunday holy instead of Saturday, as we have for every other article of our creed, namely, the authority of the Church. Whereas, you who are Protestants have really no authority for it whatever; for there is no authority for it (Sunday sacredness) in the Bible, and you will not allow that there can be authority for it anywhere else. Both you and we do, in fact, follow tradition in this matter; but we follow it believing it to be a part of God's word, and the (Catholic) Church to be its divinely appointed guardian and interpreter; you follow it (the Catholic Church), denouncing it all the time as a fallible and treacherous guide, which often 'makes the commandments of God of none effect' quoting Matthew 15:6." (The Brotherhood of St. Paul, **The Clifton Tracts**, Vol. 4, tract 4, page 15.)

"...The Church changed the observance of the Sabbath to Sunday by right of the divine, infallible authority given to her by her founder, Jesus Christ. The Protestant claiming the Bible to be the only guide of faith has no warrant for observing Sunday. In this matter the Seventh-day Adventists is the only consistent Protestant..." (**The Catholic Universe Bulletin**, August 14, 1942, page 4.)

"...Perhaps the boldest thing, the most revolutionary change the church ever did, happened in the first century. The holy day, the Sabbath, was changed from Saturday to Sunday. 'The day of the Lord' (Dies Dominica) was chosen, not from any directions noted in the Scriptures, but from the church's sense of its own power....People who think that the Scriptures should be the sole authority should logically become 7th Day Adventists, and keep Saturday holy..." (**Saint Catherine Catholic Sentinel,** May 21, 1995)

Who attempted to change God's Sabbath from the seventh day to the first day? Not God the creator who gave it. Not the prophets nor apostles who preached and taught it. Certainly it was not Our Lord and Savior, Jesus Christ, who lived it and gave it to us as an example to follow. The facts are clear. The evidence is overwhelming and unambiguous. It is the Roman Catholic Church that attempts to change God's law.

By her own prideful admission and satanically inspired boasts, she claims this dishonor. The same spirit that was manifested by Lucifer, which led him to attempt to usurp God's authority in heaven, is the same spirit that is manifested in the Roman Church when its leaders declare that they can change God's Holy word. It is the spirit of antichrist. God has given no man or organization the authority to change His law. To claim such authority is to blaspheme the name of God. That is the work of the antichrist.

As a Christian, or one of any other religious persuasion, each of us must decide whom we will worship. As humans, we will worship someone. God has placed that need to worship within us.

Your worship will be given either to the God of creation, or to a man who claims to be God and thus boasts of changing God's law.

God has given us His blessed Sabbath-day. It is an inestimable gift to us from our Creator at creation. Nowhere in God's Holy word, does He give any man the permission or authority to change His word. Nor is there any place in the Sacred record where any special significance is attached to Sunday, the first day of the week.

The Holy Bible, the only rule of faith and practice for the Christian, does not in any way sanction Sunday sacredness. We have clearly presented both the Biblical and historic evidence on who attempted the change. Now, it is your turn to make a decision. To whom will you offer your worship? Will it be to God your Creator, your Redeemer and your Sustainer; or to satan, the one who seeks to destroy your soul? Only you can decide.

The prophet Elijah declared to the people of God on Mt. Carmel,"… how long halt ye between two opinions? If the Lord be God, follow him: but if Ba-al, then follow him…" (1 Kings 18:21).

What other proof would you need to convince you that not only did God not change His law; but that He requires all men in all times to obey them. If you claim His name, then you have no choice but to obey Him and by His grace, keep holy His blessed Sabbath-day.

It is the sincere prayer of this writer that you choose God and His Holy Sabbath-day.

In our next chapter, we will provide further evidence of Rome's role in attempting to change God's law. We will trace the historical and prophetic path whereby this haughty power, attempting to take the prerogatives of God, came into existence.

CHAPTER 6

A Beast In History

The seal of God, as we have already pointed out, is His holy Sabbath-day. It is His sign of authority within His law that identifies Him as the author of the law. The Sabbath commandment has God's name and His title embodied within it. It also specifies God's sphere of authority. (Exodus 20:8-11)

We discovered also that the Sabbath is the emblem of God's everlasting covenant with all who truly believe in Him. It is God's sign between He and His people signifying that they belong to Him. (Exodus 31:15-18)

The Bible also refers to a power which, in the end of time, would have universal dominion over every nation, kindred, people and tongue. That power is referred to as **'the beast'**. The Bible further teaches that the beast will have a **'mark'** that will affect the survival of every person on planet earth.

But who is the beast and what is its mark? More importantly, however, is the question of how the beast and its mark relate to God and His seal. Whatever they are, the beast and its mark are in contradiction to God and His seal of authority, His blessed Sabbath-day.

In this chapter, we begin the process of identifying and confirming what truly is **'the beast'** and what is its **'mark'**. We willpinpoint its place in history. We will examine the part it is playing in contemporary world affairs. We will unlock the Biblical prophecies of the role of the beast and its mark in end time events. We will discover that God's holy Sabbath will be the issue most controverted in the hearts and lives of men everywhere. This will become evident as the part played by the beast and its mark become more manifest.

Some say that the mark of the beast is a computer chip that

would be implanted on the forehead or on the right hand of every inhabitant on planet earth. Others say that it will be some sort of smart card that would identify someone as being approved by the New World Order. That card, they say, will enable some to buy and sell when others can't.

As people of faith, our only true answers must come directly from the word of God. Whatever the beast and its mark are, the Bible admonishes us to be aware of them and, by God's grace, avoid them. The Bible makes it abundantly plain, that the consequences for receiving the mark of the beast are dire and deadly.

The apostle John warns, "...And the third angel followed them saying with a loud voice 'If any man worship the beast and his image, and receive his mark in his forehead or in his hand, the same shall drink of the wine of the wrath of God, which is poured out without mixture into the cup of his indignation: and he shall be tormented with fire and brimstone in the presence of the holy angels, and in the presence of the Lamb..." (Rev. 14:9-10) John again predicts a most horrific consequence for those who receive the mark of the beast. He continues, "...And the first (angel) went, and there fell a noisome and grievous sore upon men which had the mark of the beast, and upon them which worshipped his image..." (Rev. 16:2).

In both of these accounts, John is referring to the last plagues that would be poured out upon the earth. They are not mixed with God's mercy. Grace is no longer pleading for the sinner. Man's probation is closed. Jesus has declared,"...He that is unjust, let him be unjust still: and he which is filthy, let him be filthy still: and he that is righteous, let him be righteous still: and he that is holy, let him be holy still..." (Rev. 22:11) Jesus is on His glorious return to earth to rescue and redeem the righteous, and to punish the wicked and disobedient.

John reports, "...and the beast was taken, and with him the false prophet that wrought miracles before him with which he deceived them that had received the mark of the beast, and them that worshipped his image. These both were cast alive into the lake of fire burning with brimstone..." (Rev 19:20)

Quite interestingly, however, the beast does offer some benefits to those who receive his mark and worship his image. He (the beast) threatens those who refuse his authority by choosing God's seal rather than receiving his mark. John describes the conflict, "...And he (the beast) had power to give life unto the image of the beast, that the image of the beast should both speak, and cause that as many as would not worship the image of the beast should be killed...And he causeth all, both small and great, rich and poor, free and bond, to receive a mark in their right hand, or in their foreheads: And no man might buy or sell, save that he had the mark, or the name of the beast, or the number of his name..." (Rev 13:15-17).

Every human being on planet earth would have to make a choice. Either you would receive the seal of God; in which case you will suffer and perhaps die at the hand of the beast. Or, you will receive the mark of the beast, enjoy its benefits for a season, but then suffer the wrath of God as the plagues are poured out and then ultimately you will suffer eternal death. There is no middle ground. This is why it is vitally important that you know exactly, from the word of God, what truly is the beast and what is its mark.

In order to determine what is the mark of the beast, we must first identify what or who is the beast. For this we go to the word of God. It is the only reliable source for correctly identifying the beast and determining what is its mark.

The prophet Daniel tells us what is a beast. In a vision, received from God whilst in Babylonian captivity, Daniel is shown the history of the world from his time down through the ages, unto the second coming of Jesus Christ. The nations, which will become successive, dominating world powers, were represented to Daniel as 'beasts'. He relates, "...These great beasts, which are four, are four kings, which shall arise out of the earth..." (Daniel 7:17) He continues: "...The fourth beast shall be the fourth kingdom upon the earth, which shall be diverse from all kingdoms, and shall devour the whole earth, and shall tread it down and break it into pieces..." (Daniel 7:23)

God's servant not only tells us what is a beast; but he also gives us some identifying characteristics of 'the beast'. Clearly, Daniel is using a beast to denote a political power or nation. He further tells us that 'the beast' would at sometime rule the entire earth with a policy of cruelty and fierceness.

We know with certainty that Daniel's vision was from God. The Bible declares, "...And He (God) said, hear now my words. If there be a prophet among you, I the Lord will make myself known unto him in a vision, and I will speak unto him in a dream..." (Numbers 12:6).

Daniel records his dream, "...Daniel spake and said, I saw in my vision by night, and behold the four winds of the heaven strove upon the great sea... and four great beasts came up from the sea diverse one from the other..." (Daniel 7:2-3)

The beasts we have already identified as kingdoms. Daniel says that winds of heaven strove upon the sea. And what are the winds and the sea? Isaiah answers, "...Woe to the multitude of many people, which make a noise like the noise of the seas, and to the rushing of nations, that make a rushing like the rushing of mighty waters... The nations shall rush like the rushing of many: but God shall rebuke them, and they shall flee far off, and shall be chased as chaff of the mountains before the wind, and like a rolling thing before the whirlwind..." (Isaiah 17:12-13)

Daniel, like Isaiah, is thus describing the warring and strife amongst nations as they struggle against each other for political and military domination. The first beast or nation that Daniel mentions is a lion with eagles' wings. He prophesies, "...The first was like a lion and had eagles wings..." (Daniel 7:4) In prophesying about Judah's captivity into Babylon, the prophet Jeremiah declared, "...The lion is come up from ticket, and the destroyer of the Gentiles is on his way; he is gone forth from his place to make thy land desolate. And thy cities shall be laid waste without an inhabitant..." (Jeremiah 4:7). He continued, "... Behold he shall come up as clouds and his chariots shall be as a whirlwind: his horses are swifter than eagles. Woe unto us for we are spoiled..." (Jeremiah 4:13). The prophet makes it even clearer: "...And this whole land shall be a desolation and an astonishment: and these nations shall serve the king of Babylon seventy years..." (Jeremiah 25:11).

The first beast of Daniel's dream identifies unquestionably the nation of Babylon. Daniel then sees another beast (nation) coming at the first nation. "…And behold another beast, a second like unto a bear…" (Daniel 7:5).

The prophet Isaiah not only prophesied that God's people will go into captivity into Babylon; but that they will be liberated by the Persians. He records, "… That saith of Cyrus, He is my shepherd, and shall perform all my pleasure: even saying to Jerusalem, thou shalt be built, and to the temple, thy foundation shall be laid. Thus saith the Lord to his anointed, to Cyrus, whose right hand I have holden, to subdue nations before him: and I will loose the loins of kings to open before him the two leaved gates: and the gates shall not be shut…" (Isaiah 44:28, 45:1) Exactly as was prophesied, Cyrus, king of Persia, conquered the kingdom of Babylon and granted the Jewish people their release from captivity in Babylon. Cyrus' emancipation decree allowed for the Israelites to return to Jerusalem and rebuild their temple.

The scribe Ezra reports, "…Now in the first year of Cyrus, king of Persia, that the word of the Lord by the mouth of Jeremiah might be fulfilled, the Lord stirred up the Spirit of Cyrus, king of Persia, that he made a proclamation throughout all his kingdom, and put it also in writing saying: Thus saith Cyrus, king of Persia: 'The Lord God of heaven hath given me all the kingdoms of the earth: and he hath charged me to build Him an house at Jerusalem, which is at Judah…" (Ezra 1:1-2)

Cyrus, king of Persia, in his design to conquer the kingdom of Babylon, instructed his general Darius, to redirect the waters of the river Euphrates from its normal course. The river ran through the city of Babylon. The Euphrates, having been deferred from its normal flow, allowed Darius' army to enter the Babylonian capital undetected. He entered the city beneath the gates on the dry land from where the river Euphrates was redirected. That act spelled the capture of Babylon by the Medes and the Persians.

Daniel records, "…In that night was Belshazzar, the king of the Chaldeans slain and Darius the Median took the kingdom, being about three score and two years old…" (Daniel 5:30,31). The Medes were vassals of the Persians. Darius, the Median, was acting under the authority and direction of Cyrus, king of the Persians. It is thus clearly established that the second beast (nation) of Daniel's dream, represented by the bear, is none other than the empire of the Medes and Persians.

Daniel's vision continues. He next relates, "...After this, I beheld, and lo another, like a leopard, which had upon the back of it four wings of a fowl: the beast had also four heads: and dominion was given to it..." (Daniel 7:6). What nation was it that conquered the Media/Persian Empire? The historical record is undeniable.

In the latter half of 4th century BC, the Grecian conqueror and ruler, Alexander the Great, made several incursions into the Media/Persian Empire. Finally, in the fall of 331BC, he defeated Darius III, king of the Persians at the Battle of Guagamela (commonly referred to as the Battle of Arabela) This completed Alexander's conquest of the then known world. He had hitherto completed his conquest of Egypt and the rest of the then known world.

Alexander the Great, having completed this feat at the tender age of 33, did not live much longer to enjoy the fruits of his gallant victories. History records, that at a celebration at Babylon which he now ruled, Alexander worked himself into a drunken stupor. He never recovered from his drunkenness. It resulted in his death. In his dying moments, his friends asked him, "...to whom do you leave the kingdom?" To which he replied "...to the best, to the strongest..." That was exactly what happened.

Following Alexander's death, much infighting among his top generals erupted. His four strongest generals, Ptolemy Lagus, Seleucus Nicator, Cassander and Lysimachus divided up his empire among themselves.

The leopard with four wings and four heads aptly describes the swiftness and skill with which Alexander the Great conquered the world. It is also a fitting description of the subsequent dividing-up of the empire among Alexander's four strongest generals. Daniel's prophecy concerning the 3rd beast (kingdom) is thus perfectly fulfilled.

As Daniel proceeds with the account of his vision, he describes the fourth beast. He tells us, "...After this, I saw in the night vision, and behold a fourth beast dreadful and terrible, and strong exceedingly and it had great iron teeth: it devoured and brake in pieces, and stamped the residue with the feet of it: and it was diverse from all the beasts that was before it: and it had ten horns..." (Daniel 7:7).

Before we proceed with the identification of the fourth beast, it is extremely important that what has been stated thus far be clarified. Daniel's dream was given to him during the first year of the reign of Belshazzar, king of Babylon, "...In the first year of Belshazzar, king of Babylon, Daniel had a dream and visions of his head upon his bed: then he wrote the dream, and told the sum of the matters..." (Daniel 7:1)

Some three years later God again gave Daniel a vision which confirmed what he dreamt previously.

I quote from the inspired record, "...In the third year of the reign of king Belshazzar, a vision appeared unto me, even unto me Daniel, after that which appeared unto me at first..." (Daniel 8:1). It is here clearly indicated that Daniel's second dream was in connection with the first. This time however, only two beasts are portrayed.

The prophet records, "...Then I lifted up mine eyes and saw, and behold a ram which had two horns: and the horns were high: but one was higher than the other, and the higher came up last... I saw the ram pushing westward, and northward, and southward; so that no beast might stand before him, neither was there any that could deliver out of his hand, but he did according to his will, and became great..." (Daniel 8:3)

Then Daniel saw another beast (nation) coming against the first kingdom, the ram. "...And as I was considering, behold an he goat came from the west on the face of the whole earth, and touched not the ground: And the goat had a notable horn between his eyes... And he came to the ram that had the two horns, which I had seen standing before the river, and ran unto him in the fury of his power... And I saw him come close unto the ram, and he was moved with choler against him, and smote the ram, and
brake his two horns: and there was no power in the ram to stand before, but he cast him down to the ground, and stamped upon him; and there was none that could deliver the ram out of his hand... therefore the he goat waxed very great. And when he was strong the great horn was broken: and for it came up four notable ones towards the four winds of

heaven..." (Daniel 8:5-8).

Next, Daniel saw a little horn (young nation) come out of one of the four horns and ultimately grew stronger and more powerful than both the ram and the goat. Of this kingdom, Daniel writes, "...and out of one of them came forth a little horn, which waxed exceeding great, toward the south, and toward the east and toward the pleasant land... and it waxed great even to the host of heaven: and it cast down some of the host and of the stars to the ground and stamped upon them..." (Daniel 8:9,10).

In the midst of his vision, as Daniel foresaw the work of his little horn, the angel Gabriel was sent to him to give him the interpretation of the dream.

Daniel relates, "... And I heard a man's voice between the banks of the Ulai which called, and said, Gabriel, make this man to understand the vision...And he said, Behold I will make thee to know what shall be in the last end of the indignation for at the time appointed the end shall be...The Ram which thou sawest having the two horns are the kings of Media and Persia... And the rough goat is the king of Grecia: and the great horn that is between his eyes is the first king...Now that being broken, whereas four stood up for it, four kingdoms shall stand up out of the Nation, but not in his power..." (Daniel 8:21,22).

Gabriel reveals to Daniel more detail about the fourth kingdom, "...And in the latter time of their kingdom (the four horns) when transgressions are come to the full, a king of fierce countenance, and understanding dark sentences shall stand up and his power shall be mighty but not of his own power: and he shall destroy wonderful, and shall prosper and practice and shall destroy the mighty and the holy people..." (Daniel 8:23, 24).

Daniel's dreams, the second confirming the first, foretold the kingdoms that would rule the world and have significant impact upon God's people and His (God) plan of human redemption. We have clearly identified the first three beasts (kingdoms) of Daniel 7 to be (1) Babylon (2) Media /Persia and (3) Greece. We have also identified the two beasts (kingdoms) of Daniel 8 to also be Media/Persia and Greece.

These nations, beginning with Babylon, successively conquered each other to become the ruling world power of their time. Each conquered more territory and dominated more people than the one preceding it.

Babylon ruled from 606BC to 536BC. It was followed by Media/Persia, which ruled from 536BC to 331BC. Media / Persia was conquered by Alexander the Great. The Grecian empire extended from 331BC to about 168BC. These are documented historical facts.

But who is the nation that followed them? What nation is the fourth beast of Daniel 7 and the king of fierce countenance (the little horn) of Daniel 8? Since the dream of Daniel 7 is consistent with the vision of Daniel 8, then the nations portrayed by these symbols must also be identical. We have already settled the matter with regards to Babylon, Media/Persia, and Greece.

In the next chapter, we will positively identify the fourth beast / king of fierce countenance (the little horn), which represents the nation that would rise after the Grecian empire. As we continue to identify this beast, you will discover that it is the same beast (kingdom) that is spoken of in the book of Revelation. (Chapter 13:1-10) We will then proceed to reveal what is its mark and how it affects God's people and impacts His holy Sabbath.

CHAPTER 7

The Beast and It's Mark Identified

In our last chapter, we presented the historical background pertaining to the beast. We showed that from a Biblical perspective, the term 'beast' actually represents a nation or kingdom. Also, we showed that a kingdom or a nation is sometimes represented as a horn. With that perspective in mind, let's discover who is '**The Beast**' and what is its '**Mark**'.

Following the world rule of Greece, and the dividing-up of Alexander the Great's empire by his four most powerful generals, history records the rapid rise of a small, seemingly insignificant tribe coming out from banks of the river Tiber. It rose with swiftness and might to become the world's dominating power in less than 200 years.

Legends abound about the birth and formative years of this nation. What is not in doubt, nor is at all legend, is her rise to world greatness and dominance. According to God's word, that kingdom will rise, after a time of seeming inactivity, to rule the world once again in the last days of earth's history. Her resurgence to world dominance will last until the second coming of Our Lord and Savior Jesus Christ.

As she rises to universal power, that kingdom will enforce its mark of authority upon all men on planet earth. All will submit to her authority. Except those, who by faith, receive the seal of authority of the God of creation. That kingdom and its mark we will now unveil.

The prophet Daniel, in Daniel 7:7, (quoted earlier) describes a nation that was unlike anything he had seen previously in his vision. It was a mighty nation with immense military power. It conquered all the other kingdoms that were before it to ascend to the rulership of the world. It moved with swiftness, cruelty and determined fierceness to crush its opponents and control its conquered prey.

Likewise, in his vision of Daniel 8, the prophet refers to the same kingdom thus, "...and out of one of them (the four divisions of Alexander the Great's Greek Empire/the he goat) came forth a little horn, which waxed exceeding great, toward the south and toward the east, and toward the pleasant land (Daniel 8:9) Historical evidence supports the fact that the Roman empire was the dominating power that arose after the Grecian empire. Rome extended its power to the south (Egypt), to the east (Macedonia), and to the 'pleasant land' (Palestine) No other power matches this description.

The characteristics of the fourth beast are synonymous, in every particular, with one entity and one entity only. That is the Roman empire.First in its pagan form and then its Papal form. It is the only nation that rose from obscurity to rule the world with a mighty fist for more than 600 years. Rome indeed grew exceedingly great and stood up to the 'Prince of the host' (Jesus Christ). It was the Roman Empire, in its pagan form, that crucified our Savior and destroyed the Jewish temple. In its papal form, it caused the heavenly sanctuary to be 'cast down' by instituting a system of earthly priests in the place of our Heavenly High Priest, Jesus Christ. It is a historical fact that the Roman empire arose out of the divided Greek empire to rule the world with an iron fist. Imperial Rome is, without a doubt, the kingdom that followed the world reign of Greece.

The history of the Roman people can be traced back to more than 1000 years BC. But, it is their bloody victories in the Punic wars, culminating in their conquest of Spain, North Africa, Greece, Asia Minor and Egypt that established Rome as a world empire around the year 149 BC. This is the nation that is brought to view in Daniel's dream of Daniel 7:7, and his vision of Daniel 8:9, quoted earlier.

The conquests of Imperial Rome were magnanimous. They are thus aptly described by the prophet. Any challenge to her supremacy was swiftly subdued. All opposition to her authority was eradicated. The strong arm of her legendary military might was uncontestable.

Daniel continues, "...I considered the horns, and behold, there came up among them another little horn, before whom there were three of the first horns plucked up by the roots; and, behold, in this horn were eyes like the eyes of man, and a mouth speaking great things..." (Daniel 7:8)

He reiterates this series of events in his vision of Daniel 8. He relates, "... And it waxed great, even to the host of heaven; and it cast down some of the host and of the stars to the ground, and stamped upon them...he magnified himself even to the Prince of the host, and by him the daily was taken away and the place of his sanctuary was cast down... And in the latter time of their kingdom, when the transgressions are come to the full, a king of fierce countenance, and understanding dark sentences, shall stand up...and his power shall be mighty but not by his own power: and he shall destroy wonderfully, and shall prosper and practice, and shall destroy the mighty and holy people..." (Daniel 8: 10, 11, 12, 23, 24)

In both of these accounts, Daniel is portraying a change in the nature of this kingdom. It is a change from its militaristic nature to one of a religious nature. This is especially true and accurate of the Roman empire. Rome's transformation from a world military might into the world's most dominant religion of its time is undeniable.

Historian Will Durant writes, "... When Christianity conquered Rome, the ecclesiastical structure of the pagan church, the title and vestments of the Pontifex Maximus, the worship of the Great Mother goddess and a multitude of comforting divinities... the joy and solemnity of old festivals, and the pageantry of immemorial ceremony, passed like maternal blood into the new religion, and captive Rome captured her conqueror. The reigns and skills of government were handed down by a dying empire to a virile Papacy. The lost power of the broken sword was re-won by the magic of the consoling word. The armies of the state were replaced by the missionaries of the church, moving in all directions along the Roman roads; and the revolted provinces, accepting Christianity, again acknowledged the sovereignty of Rome. The church with the shadow of the ancient authority behind it, was the only symbol left of imperial Rome. Its bishop, the pope of Rome, was the city's only recourse for leadership and protection. The Roman Empire in Europe would be replaced by the spiritual empire, which came to be temporal as well, whose reigning seigneur was the bishop of Rome…" (**Caesar and Christ**, page 672)

Unlike the previous world kingdoms (Babylon, Media/Persia and Greece), the Roman Empire was not conquered by another world power. It changed structure from pagan Rome to Papal Rome. This is what Daniel sees as he reports on the fourth beast having ten horns. (Daniel 7: 7,8)

The pagan Roman empire reached it's zenith in about the fourth century AD. It began to loosen its military and political grip on the nations that comprised the empire. The empire's decline was troubled and slow, bottoming out about 476 AD.

As the pagan empire declined, the church grew more and more powerful to become the Papal empire. Historian Alexander C. Flick records, "…The mighty Catholic Church was little more than the Roman empire baptized. Rome was transformed as well as converted. It is not a matter of great surprise, therefore, to find that from the first to the fourth century, the church had undergone many changes…" (**Rise of the Medieval Church, page 148,149**)

Rome's resources and attention were now directed towards resisting the marauding barbarian tribes in her midst. These tribes grew more and more independent of the seat of power in Rome. Eventually, they carved up the empire unto ten divisions, loosely connected to the imperial monarchy. The empire was eventually divided into the eastern half and the western half.

The western empire, today known as Western Europe, was for all intents and purposes, under the control of the church. Such developments allowed for the further political independence of those tribes comprising the Western Empire. What kept them together was the burgeoning influence and authority of the church. What military might and political strategy failed to accomplish, the religion of the church achieved.

Below are those tribes with their corresponding modern names:

Visigoths – Spain

Lombards - Italy
Anglo Saxons - England
Franks – France
Alemani – Germany
Burgundians – Switzerland
Suevi – Portugal
Heruli – Uprooted. No modern counterpart
Ostrogoths – Uprooted. No modern counterpart
Vandals – Uprooted. No modern counterpart.

    Even as the military might of Rome was waning and its political strength disintegrating, the increasingly powerful church provided the glue that held the nations together. That glue was religion. From the time of Constantine's supposed acceptance of Christianity, in the early 4th century, the pure religion of Christ was amalgamated with prevailing, customary pagan religious practices. This mix of Christianity and paganism was advanced by the use of what military strength was retained by the individual tribes. Foremost in support of the church and its religion was the Franks and their king, Clovis.

    Of the ten emerging nations of the former unified empire, three – Heruli, Vandals and Ostroghoths, opposed the teachings and authority of the burgeoning church. They followed the leadings of Arius, a bishop of Alexandria, Egypt who refused to accept, among other things, the church's teaching of the Trinity and the Divinity Of Jesus Christ. For these reasons, those three nations were rooted up by the church, utilizing the military force of those who agreed with her and were under her control.

    Such is represented by Daniel's account of the little horn that uprooted three of the ten horns. (Daniel 7:8) That little horn is representative of the emerging church. It not only filled the vacuum left by the declining pagan empire; but it grew to become even more powerful and vicious. The last one of those nations/horns, the Ostrogoths, was obliterated and vanished from Rome and the history books in 538 AD.

    The emperor Justinian, having had the laws of the empire

rewritten to accommodate the growing power of the church, finally ceded full and complete control to her in that very year. This marked the transfer from political/military Rome to Papal Rome, today called the Papacy.

What the Caesars could not achieve through military might and political scheming, the Papacy accomplished though the force of apostate religion, i.e. reunification of the nations of Western Europe.

Daniel details the workings and development of the little horn (the Papacy). "...And of the ten horns that were in his head, and of the other which came up, and before whom three fell: even of that horn that had eyes, and a mouth that spoke very great things, whose look was more stout than his fellows... I beheld and the same horn made war with the saints and prevailed against them, until the Ancient of days come and judgment was given to the saints of the Most High and the time came that the saints possessed the kingdom. ...And he (the little horn/the Papacy) shall speak great words against the most High, and shall wear out the saints of the most High and think to change times and laws; and they shall be given into his hand until a time and times the dividing of time..." (Daniel 7: 20,21,22, 25)

Here is a summary of Daniel's description and the historical record of the little horn that emerged from the divided fourth kingdom. It would up-root three of the ten horns/nations of divided Rome (Daniel 7:8). It would have at its head, a man who speaks for it and has full authority over it. (Daniel 7:8, 20) It would be diverse (different) from the other ten horns (Daniel 7:24) It would persecute God's people (Daniel 7:25) It would speak great words (blaspheme) against God (Daniel 7:25). It would attempt to change God's law (Daniel 7:25).

These points of identification are an accurate description of one entity alone. That entity is the medieval Roman Church. It is today known as the Roman Catholic Church. This is the **'BEAST'**. This is the antichrist power of Bible prophecy. This is perhaps shocking, but true. Both the historical record and Biblical prophecy confirm this fact.

It must be carefully noted here that the above characterization does not apply to the tens of millions of godly people who sincerely believe they are serving God by being part of this organization. We are referring to a system and hierarchy whose history conforms to the facts presented.

The apostle John picks up the story. The little horn, previously described as the Papacy or Roman Catholic Church is now presented to the apostle John in his vision from the Mount of Patmos. He writes, "... And I stood upon the sand of the sea, and saw a **beast** rise up out of the sea, having seven heads and ten horns, and upon his horns ten crowns, and upon his heads the name of blasphemy..." (Revelation 13:1)

As pointed out earlier, the sea or waters represents people. The Scripture again explains, "...The waters which thou sawest, where the whore sitteth, are peoples, and multitudes, and nations, and tongues..." (Revelation 17:15) Clearly, this is an indication that this beast/nation is emerging from a populated area of the world and is ruling over many people.

John goes on to state that the beast had seven heads and ten horns. Again, Scripture plainly explains what those seven heads are. John writes again, "...and here is the mind which hath wisdom. The seven heads are seven mountains, on which the woman sits..." (Revelation 17:9) Our attention is now focused upon the woman who sits on seven hills. But who is this woman?

The Bible clearly points out that a woman is a religious body. Referring to the true church of Jesus Christ, the apostle John declares,"... let us be glad and rejoice, and give honor to Him: for the marriage of the Lamb is come, and his wife hath made herself ready..." (Revelation 19:7) The prophet Jeremiah agrees, "...I have likened the daughter of Zion (God's church) to a comely and delicate woman..." (Jeremiah 6:2).

The woman we recognize as being a church. But, we must take careful note that the woman referred to by John is definitely not God's church. She is neither comely nor delicate. She is not dressed as a bride. In fact, John describes this church that is located on seven hills, as a whore. (Revelation 17: 15) quoted above.

John elaborates, "...And the woman was arrayed in purple and scarlet color, and decked with gold and precious stones and pearls, having a golden cup in her hand full of abominations and filthiness of her fornication. And upon her forehead was the name written, MYSTERY BABYLON THE GREAT, THE MOTHER OF HARLOTS AND ABOMINATIONS OF THE EARTH. And I saw the woman drunken with the blood of the saints, and with the blood of the martyrs of Jesus: and when I saw her, I wondered with great admiration…" (Revelation 17: 4 - 6).

This woman (church) is exceedingly rich in worldly goods. She promotes anti-Christian doctrines under the cloak of Christian piety. She also persecutes God's people.

Theologian and historian Alexander Hislop, in his classic, **Two Babylons**, states, "…There has never been any difficulty in the mind of any enlightened Protestant in identifying the woman sitting on seven mountains and having on her forehead the name, "Mystery Babylon the Great," with the Roman apostasy. No other city in the world has ever been celebrated, as the city of Rome has, for its situation on seven hills. Pagan poets and orators, who had not thought of elucidating prophecy, have alike characterized it as the 'Seven Hilled City'. Thus, Virgil refers to it, '…Rome has both the most beautiful city in the world, and alone has surrounded for herself seven heights with a wall…"

He continues, "… Properitius, in the same strain, speaks of it (only adding another trait, which completes the apocalyptic picture) as 'the lofty city on seven hills, which governs the whole world'. This is a just counterpart of the divine statement: ' the woman which reigneth over the kings of the earth' (Revelation 17: 18).

Hislop goes further. "… To call Rome the city of seven hills was by its citizens, held to be descriptive as to call it by its own proper name. Hence Horacespeaks of it by reference to its seven hills alone, when he addresses:'…The Gods who have set their affections on the seven hills...'Martial, in like manner, speaks of "…the seven dominating mountains…"

Unquestionably, therefore, the seven heads is referring to the religious aspect of the beast/nation. It denotes the ecclesiastical arm of the papacy. Now, we focus on the ten horns.

John explains, "…And the ten horns which thou saw are ten kings, which have received no kingdom as yet; but receive power as kings one hour with the beast…These have one mind, and shall give their power and strength unto the beast..." (Revelation 17:12-13)

The ten horns clearly represent the political / military powers that align themselves with the Papacy. These allow the church to rule over them. Whether in a historical perspective, as in the ten divisions of the Imperial Roman empire; or in the contemporary political climate, where the United Nations and the Club of Rome have divided up the entire world into ten economic districts, the identification of the ten horns, as the political/military complement of the Papacy is equally fitting. The point remains that we are looking, in either case, at a universal church/state union, in which the church is ruling the state.

This description perfectly complements the characterization given in Revelation 17:3. "... So he carried me away in the wilderness: and I saw a woman sit upon a scarlet colored beast, full of names of blasphemy, having seven heads and ten horns..."

John, like Daniel, refers to the element of blasphemy connected to this power. Blasphemy is a religious term. It implies speaking against the God of creation or purporting to take the prerogatives of His office.

For example, we find that Jesus, having healed a man from his paralytic condition, proceeded to forgive his sins. Luke reports, "...And when He (Jesus) saw their faith, He said unto him:' man, thy sins are forgiven thee'. And the Scribes and the Pharisees began to reason, saying who is this, which speaks blasphemies? Who can forgive sins, but God alone?"(Luke 5:21)

Of course, Jesus was not speaking blasphemy. He was verily God in the flesh. Therefore, the privilege to forgive men of their sins is exclusively His. The idea of claiming to forgive other men of their sins is the prerogative of God and God only.

Jesus also declared, "...Me and my Father are one..." (John 10:30). The Jews reacted to this by taking up stones to stone Jesus to death. What was their reason? John reports, "...The Jews answered him saying, 'for a good work we stone thee not: but for blasphemy; and because that thou, being a man makes thyself God'..." (John 10:30)

But the church on the seven hills teaches, "...The Pope is not only the representative of Jesus Christ, but he is Jesus Christ Himself, hidden under the veil of flesh" (**The Catholic Standard**, July 1895). She continues: "...When the pope is crowned, he is reminded that he is the father of princess, and kings, and the supreme ruler of the universe, and on the earth, the vicar of Jesus Christ our Savior, and the Governor of the world..."(Lucius Ferraris, **Ecclesiastical Dictionary,** 1763)

Notice the declaration regarding the Roman Catholic priesthood, "...The Priest holds the place of the Savior himself, when, by saying "ego te absolvo" (I thee absolve), he absolves from sin...to pardon a single sin requires all the omnipotence of God...But what only God can do by His omnipotence, the priest can do by saying 'ego te absolvo a peccatis tuis'..." **(Dignities and Duties of the Priest, pages 34, 36)**

Further, the woman on the seven mountains claims, "...Thus the priest in a certain manner, be called the creator of his creator. The power of the priest is the power of the divine person; for the transubstantiation of the bread requires as much power as the creation of the world..." (**ibid.** pages 32, 33).

One can hardly get any more blasphemous than that. Such is the nature of the beast. These are the pronouncements of the Church of Rome.

John continues, "...And the beast which I saw was like unto a leopard, and his feet were the feet of a bear, and the mouth as the mouth of a lion: and the dragon gave him his power, and his seat, and great authority..." (Revelation 13:2)

Here, John is describing the Papacy as having the religious characteristics and embodying the practices of the world's ruling powers that immediately preceded her.

Looking back down the prophetic timeline, John sees this antichrist power as possessing and practicing the policies, beliefs and dogmas of Greece (the leopard), Media/Persia (the bear) and Babylon (the lion) These were the nations that ruled, in reverse succession, before the Roman Empire. (Daniel 7:4-7)

Daniel also confirms this fact. He declares, "...As concerning the rest of the beasts they had their dominion taken away: yet their lives were prolonged for a season and time..." (Daniel 7:12) In other words, both Daniel and John are saying that the religious and political elements of Babylon, Media/Persia and Greece were adopted into the Roman empire, and ultimately amalgamated into the Papacy.

Most strikingly however, John not only declares that all the abominations of the previous world empires reside in the Papacy; but he also states that she gets her power and authority from the dragon. And who is the dragon? Inspiration answers, "...And the great dragon was cast out, that old serpent, called the devil, and satan (Revelation 12:9).

The Papacy, the Bible explains, gets its power and authority from the devil himself. Like satan, all its schemes are but a masterpiece of deception designed to usurp the authority of God in men's hearts. It seeks to receive the worship of men that only God deserves.

In further describing the Papacy, John relates, "...And I saw one of his heads as it were wounded to death; and his deadly wound was healed; and all the world wondered after the beast...And they worshiped the dragon which gave power unto the beast; and they worshiped the beast saying, who is like unto the beast? Who is able to make war with him...." (Revelation 13:3,4).

The wound is, at least in part, an obvious reference to the great Protestant Reformation. This Bible-based, Holy-Spirit led, opposition movement posed a formidable challenge to the universal reign of the Papacy with her pagan traditions and spurious religious doctrines. More precisely, however, the deadly wound refers to the dismantling of the Papacy under Napoleon Bonaparte.

The year was 1798. Napoleon, utterly disgusted with the domination of the church and determined to conquer the world, sent his most-able general, Louis Berthier, into the city of Rome. The then ruling Pope, Pope Pius VI was taken prisoner by Berthier and exiled to Valence, France where he (Pope Pius VI) died in 1799. In effect, what Napoleon accomplished was the taking away of the political/military power from the Papacy. He declared it to be a religious entity only. By this act, Napoleon separated the church from the states. That act constituted the deadly wound - the separation of the political/military from the ecclesiastical. Slowly, but stealthily, the Papacy set out to regain its lost position as ruler of the nations. The healing of the wound manifested in earnest in February 1929. In that year, the Roman Church signed an agreement with Premier Benito Mussolini of Italy.

He was one of her most faithful and dedicated sons. The agreement is named the Lateran Treaty.

That action effectively restored the political power of the Papacy by declaring it a nation unto itself. Of course, it always retained its seemingly religious character.

The Associated Press headlined the occasion, "...Mussolini and Gasparri sign historic Roman Pact...heal wound of many years..." The story, appearing on February 11, 1929 stated, "...The Roman question tonight was a thing of the past and the Vatican was at peace with Italy. The formal accomplishment of this today, was the exchange of signatures in the historic palace of St. John Lateran by two noteworthy plenipotentiaries, Cardinal Gasparri for Pope Pius XI and Premier Mussolini for King Emmanuel III..."

The San Francisco Chronicle reported on February 12, 1929, "...In affixing the autographs to the memorable document, **healing the wound** which has festered since 1870, extreme cordiality, was displayed on both sides...."

It is breathtakingly remarkable that secular news sources, with no reference to Biblical prophecy, used the very words of Scripture to describe the reemergence of the Papacy as a world political entity.

Who can doubt that since that time, the Roman Church has grown rapidly into a dominant world political player. Her religious influence has permeated every corner of the world. Presidents and kings, princes and prime ministers, men and women everywhere bow down in blind obedience and reverence to the Pope of Rome. The late Pope John Paul 11 epitomized this phenomenon best as he traveled from country to country, promoting the persona of the most trusted, pious religious leader in the world.

How sad is it that Christians everywhere, while claiming Jesus as their Savior, are bowing down and worshiping the Pope of Rome as their Lord. As pointed out earlier, that is what Sunday sacredness is... servitude to the Pope of Rome.

The apostle Paul reminds us, "...Know ye not, that to whom ye yield yourselves servants to obey, his servants ye are to whom ye obey; whether of sin unto death, or of obedience unto righteousness?..."

(Romans 16:16).

We worship God by keeping His commandments. Jesus declares, "...If ye love me, keep my commandments..." (John 14:15). The wise man Solomon agrees, "...Let us hear the conclusion of the whole matter: Fear God, and keep His commandments; for his is the whole duty of man..." (Ecclesiastes 12:13).

God has given us His Ten Commandments. He requires us to keep them all. This includes keeping holy His Sabbath-day, the 7th day of the week. God calls His Sabbath-day a sign between He and His people (Exodus 31:17). It is the seal of His law in which He places Hs name, His title and His territory of rulership. (Exodus 20: 8-11)

Roman Catholicism, the antichrist power of Bible prophecy, says not so. She declares, exactly as Daniel prophesied in Daniel 7:25, that she would attempt to change God's law. She declares that that change is her mark of authority.

In the **Converts Catholicism,** the Roman Catholic premier teaching source of her followers, we find the following:

Question: Which is the Sabbath day
Answer: Saturday is the Sabbath-day.
Question: Why do we observe Sunday instead of Saturday.
Answer: We observe Sunday instead of Saturday because the Catholic Church transferred the solemnity from Saturday to Sunday.

God authorizes no such transfer in His word. Such blasphemous declarations are manifestations of the spirit of antichrist who seeks to take the place of Christ.

Men may try, but it is impossible to change God's law. The audacity of this power, under the influence of the devil himself (Revelation 13:2) has led the Papacy to make this boastful claim.

She affirms,"...Of course, the Catholic church claims that the change was her act. And the act is a '**MARK**' of her ecclesiastical power and authority in religious matters..." (**Letter from Cardinal James Gibbons of Baltimore**)

She continues, "...Sunday is our **MARK** of authority. The

church is above the Bible, and this transference of Sabbath observance is proof of that fact...." (**The Catholic Record,** September 1, 1929)

Furthermore, the late Pope John Paul II declared in His apostolic letter of July 1998, "...The celebration of the Christian Sunday remains on the threshold of the third millennium, an indispensable element of our Christian identity..." (Section 30, **Dies Domini**)

God says that the Sabbath is the sign of His authority. His inspired word reveals no concept of a Christian Sunday. That is the mark of apostasy. The Pope says Sunday is the mark of his authority. The question is: whom are you following?

The Pope further issued a not so veiled threat to those who do not go along with his Sunday command, "...Christians will naturally strive to ensure that civil legislation respects their duty to keep Sabbath (Sunday) holy..." (Section 67, **ibid.**)

The plain fact is that only God can make a day holy. The day He has made holy is the seventh day, today called Saturday. It is the only, holy Sabbath-day.

Make no mistake, this legislation attempting to establish Sunday in place of God's Sabbath will be implemented around the world. Its violation will be punishable by imprisonment and death. The church has declared that anyone not abiding by her Sunday decree will be treated as a heretic. You need only to take a look at her past history to see how heretics were treated. They were burned alive at the stake, quartered at the rack, boiled in oil, fed to hungry, wild animals, fed to rats, beheaded at the guillotine and subjected to other devilish devices too numerous to mention.

Such actions characterizes church's actions of old. She has not changed the dogmas that led to such atrocities. She will not hesitate to do them again when vantage ground is granted to her.

Contrary to her public persona, the Church of Rome has not changed. She covers the iron hand of persecution with the velvet glove of religion. Her spirit of religious intolerance and insatiable lust for world domination are the underpinnings of her aims and purposes.

"...That the Church of Rome has shed more innocent blood than any other institution that have ever existed among mankind, will be questioned by no Protestant who has a competent knowledge of history... It is impossible to form a complete conception of the multitude of her victims, and it is quite certain that no powers of imagination can adequately realize their sufferings..." (W.E.H. Lecky, **History of The Rise and Influence of The Spirit of Rationalism in Europe,** Volume 2, page 32, 1910 ed)

Pope John Paul's declaration in Dies Domini is no empty threat. When the Papacy will have once again orchestrated its rise to the governorship of the world, then all will know the true nature of the beast. Then all will have to choose. Your choice will have to be between the God of creation and His holy Sabbath-day (His seal), and the Pope of Rome, who claims to be God with his Sunday sacredness. (his mark)

The final, and perhaps most revealing trait of the beast, is John's characterization of its leader. He declares, "...Here is wisdom. Let him that hath understanding count the number of the beast: for it is the number of a man; and his number is six hundred three score and six..." (Revelation 13:18). That is 666.

When someone is elected pope, he is crowned with a crown upon which is inscribed – VICARIUS FILII DEI. The numerical equivalent of that Roman title is as follows:

$$V-5, I-1, C-100, A-0, R-0, I-1, U-5, S-0 = 112$$
$$F-0, I-1, L-50, I-1, I-1 = 53$$
$$D-500, E-0, I-1 = 501$$

Total 666

How remarkable. The Pope is referred to as the Vicar of Christ. This title is translated to mean He who takes the place of God. And who is it that Isaiah says seeks to take the place of God? (Isaiah 14:12-17)

The prophet declares that it is the devil, the antichrist. The identification of **'the beast'** is complete, accurate and undeniable.

The Protestant Reformers recognized this power to be exactly what the Bible declares it to be, the anti-Christ of Bible prophecy. Martin Luther declared, "...We here are of the conviction that the Papacy is the seat of the true and real anti-Christ... personally I declare that I owe the pope no other obedience than that to anti-Christ..." **(Prophetic Faith of our Fathers,** Vol. 2.pg 121 by LeRoy Edwin Froom)

John Wesley agrees, "... He (the pope) is in an emphatic sense, the Man of Sin, as he increases all manner of sin above measure. And so he is, too, properly styled The Son of Perdition as he has caused the death of numberless multitudes, both of his opposers and followers. He it is that exalteth himself above all that is called Christ, or that is worshipped... claiming the highest power and highest honor... claiming the prerogatives which belong to God alone..." (**Antichrist and his Ten Kingdoms,** pg 110, John Wesley)

John Calvin joins the chorus, "...Some persons think us too severe and censorious when we call the Roman pontiff anti-Christ. But those who are of this opinion do not consider that they bring the same charge of presumption against Paul himself, after whom we speak and whose language we adopt... I shall briefly show that Paul's words in 2 Thessalonians 2 are not capable of any other interpretation than that which applies to the Papacy..." (**Institutes,** John Calvin)

The sentiments expressed by Luther, Wesley and Calvin were identical to those of John Knox of Scotland, Thomas Cramer of England, Roger Williams of the United States and the entire Protestant Reformation movement. It is too sad that Christians today have not only lost sight of the Reformation; but are seeking the aid of the Papacy in their zeal to have the government institute religious laws.

Now that we have identified the beast (the anti-Christ) and its mark (Sunday sacredness); we'll next look at America, the Sabbath and the prophetic role this nation is fulfilling in the world today.

CHAPTER 8
America And The Sabbath

In our last few chapters, we identified, both from secular history and Biblical prophecy, what is the '**Beast**' and what is its '**Mark**'. The evidence points conclusively to the beast being the Papacy (The Roman Catholic Church) and her mark being Sunday sacredness.

The apostle John, in the thirteenth chapter of the Book of Revelation, gives us clearer evidence of the time of rule of Roman Catholicism. We discussed in the previous chapter, that in the year 1798, its reign came to a halt. This was at the hands of Napoleon's general Louis Berthier. He marched into Rome, arrested Pope Puis VI, and exiled him to Valence, France.

This, we proved, constituted the deadly wound. The healing of the wound was shown to be the agreement made between Premier Mussolini of Italy and the Papacy.

John the Revelator re-emphasizes the point of the wounding of the beast. He states, "…He that leadeth into captivity, shall go into captivity: he that killeth with the sword, must be killed with the sword: Here is the patience (comfort) and the faith of the Saints…" (Revelation13: 10).

Just about the time that the beast from the sea (Revelation 13:1/Roman Catholicism arising out of the populated areas of Western Europe) is wounded (loses its political ability), John reports that another beast (nation) arises from the earth. But what nation does this earth-beast represent?

John continues, "…And I beheld another beast, coming out of the earth and he had two horns like a lamb and he spoke as a dragon…" (Revelation13: 11)

The sea, we have already pointed out, represents people, nations and tongues. This is a reference to a well-populated area of the world. All the nations, that we have thus far discussed, arose from populated areas and ascended to the world stage through strife and conquest. But this nation comes out of the earth. This is in contrast to the nations that came out of the sea. The only justifiable conclusion that can be drawn about this nation is that it arose out of an unpopulated area of the world.

Of all the other nations mentioned by Daniel and John, none is referred to as having as part of their character, a notion of worshipping the true God. This nation, coming out of the earth, however, is described as having two horns like a lamb.

A lamb in Scripture refers to Jesus. The apostle John, referring to Jesus, at the time of His (Jesus) baptism, records, "...The next day John saw Jesus coming unto him, and said 'Behold the Lamb of God, which takes away the sin of the world..." (John 1:29)

The idea of Revelation 13:11, as presented by John, is that of a nation professing Christian qualities and arising out of an unpopulated area. John also places the birth of this nation in the time frame of the demise of the Papacy.

There is one nation and one nation only that fits these specifications. That nation is undoubtedly the United States of America.

John Wesley writes of the nation that was to arise after the Papacy, "...He has not yet come, though be cannot be afar off. For he is to appear at the end of the forty-two months of the first beast..." **(Explanatory Notes on the New Testament,** page 735, John Wesley).

The forty-two months is in reality 1260 years, extending from 538 AD to 1798 AD. We have already established this period to be the time period of Roman Catholicism's dark reign over the world.

Forty-two prophetic months (1260 days) is equivalent to 1260 literal years (30 days per month x 42 months).

The prophet Moses explains, "...After the number of the days in which ye searched the land, even forty days, each day for a year, shall ye bear your iniquities, even forty years, and ye shall know my breach of promise..." (Numbers 14:34) (See also Ezekiel 4:6).

Utilizing this prophetic yardstick, we clearly see the prophetic accuracy of the reign of the Papacy. It was officially established in 538 AD when Emperor Justinian decreed the Catholic church to have complete control over the empire. Its rule extended to 1798 AD, when Napoleon's general, Berthier, deposed Pope Pius VI. This period is precisely 1260 years.

John the Revelator also confirms this time period. In referring to the period of Papal persecution of God's people, he writes, "...And the woman (the true church) fled into the wilderness, where she hath a place prepared of God, that they should feed her for a thousand, two hundred and three score days..." (Revelation 12:6) This is exactly as the Scriptures foretold it to be, 1260 years.

When we consider the events that gave birth to the United States of America, the accuracy of this prophecy is undeniably accurate and fascinating. The struggle of the American Colonies for independence began in 1775. In 1776 the Declaration of Independence was signed and the founding fathers declared the United States of America to be an independent nation. In 1777 the Articles of Confederation were adopted. In 1787 the U.S. Constitution was framed. On July 26, 1788 it was ratified by the original 13 states. On the first of March 1789, the U.S. Constitution went into effect.

This was all taking place as the Papacy was loosening its hold on the people of the world. The United States was emerging not only as a new nation, but also as a bastion of freedom for those who were fleeing the pangs of popery.

People fled Europe by the thousands. They sought to find a nation without a Pope and a country without a king. They risked their very lives to move to a country in which they would not have to be enslaved by the dogmas of the Pope and his church, or be controlled by the tyranny of kings and princes who persecuted them on behalf of the Pope.

George Alfred Townsend writes, "...the history of the United States was separated by a beneficent providence far from this wild and cruel history of the rest of the continent..." (**The New World Compared With The New,** page 633)

Charles Summer wrote the following words in an article in the **Atlantic Monthly** of September 1886. He described the emergence of the United States of America thus, "...A revolution that has stranger marks of divine interposition, superseding the ordinary course of human affairs, than any other event which the world had experienced…"

The ordinary course of human affairs by which nations rise to power is through war, strife and military conquest. Nothing of the sort characterized America's birth as a nation.

America was born as a nation that provided a sanctuary for those fleeing political and religious persecution from the kings and popes of Europe.

Such was the rise of America. In addition to its youthfulness, apparent harmlessness and seeming Christian character, John declares that this nation would one day speak like a dragon. He also portrays this emerging nation as having two horns like a lamb.

As was earlier pointed out, horns represent nations and kingdoms. Those nations exercised certain powers over their inhabitants and others within their spheres of influence.

From the rendering of horns in this instance, it is clear that the reference is more akin to the power, influence, and strength of the nation rather than to the nation itself. For the record has already declared that it was one beast (nation) and not two nations to be represented by the two horns. Notice also, that unlike the beast from the sea, the beast from the earth has no crowns upon its horns. This denotes the lack of kingly or ecclesiastical authority over the inhabitants of the new nation.

Nevertheless, John is in effect referring to the source of strength of this earth nation. We have, quite accurately, identified this nation to be the United States of America.

And where does the power and strength of America lie? It is in her Constitution. America's strength lies in her people who operate under the precepts of what James Madison calls "…The sacred ark of the people's covenant…"

The very first amendment of the U.S. Constitution reads thus, "…Congress shall make no law, respecting the establishment of religion or prohibiting the free exercise thereof, or abridging the freedom of speech, or of the press; or the right of the people peaceably to assembly and to petition the government for a redress of grievances…"

More than anything else, this is what gives power and strength to the American ideal. It is the very foundation of the American experience. This is what is symbolized by the two horns of Revelation 13:11.

On one hand we have the guarantee of freedom of religion. Those that fled the persecuting power of the first beast (the Papacy) came to a land where they can worship God according to the dictates of their own consciences.

Edward Everett in a speech made at Plymouth, Maine on December 22, 1824 declared, "...Did they look for a retired spot, inoffensive for its obscurity, and safe in its remoteness, where the little church of Leyden might enjoy the freedom of conscience? Behold the might over which, in peaceful conquest, victory without strife, they have borne the banner of the cross..."

This is a conclusive and irrefutable interpretation of John's dream. Religious Liberty is one of the foundational pillars of our nation, the United States of America. Thus John symbolizes it as one of the horns on the lamb-like beast rising up out of the earth. It is one of the two sources of power of the American experiment.

The other horn is equally important. It represents the other source of America's strength. In it is symbolized the other great foundational principle of these United States i.e. Republicanism. This idea suggests a government for the people, of the people and by the people. It further guarantees the respect of minority rights within the context of majority rule. It is in stark contrast to the lands of Europe from which so many fled to make America their home. The idea of a country without a king and a church without a pope was one for which men and women were willing to risk all their earthly possessions, including their lives.

The Constitution of the United States afforded the immigrants of Europe just that. Article IV Section 4 reads, "...The United States shall guarantee to every state in this union a Republican form of government..." Article VI reads, "...No religious test shall ever be required as a qualification to any office of public trust under the United States..."

These revolutionary concepts were uniquely American. They were conceived and implemented as bulwarks against the incursion of papal principles into the new nation. It was as if Omnipotence had ordained the United States of America to be a divine oasis in His grand plan for the redemption of men's souls.

But what John sees afterward is quite shocking. He states that this nation, the United States of America, the lamb like beast with two horns, will one day speak like a dragon. He continues, "...and he (the lamb- like beast) exercises all the power of the first beast before him, and causes the earth and them which dwell therein to worship the first beast, whose deadly wound was healed..."(Revelation 13: 12).

In the previous chapter, it was made clear that the dragon is Satan, the devil (Revelation 12:9). It was also pointed out that the Papacy, the world power before the rise of the United States, operated under the influence of the devil (Revelation 13:2).

Amazingly, we now find that the United States will not only speak like the dragon (enact laws that deprive men and women of their God given and constitutionally confirmed freedoms); but it will force the entire world to worship the Papacy, which is in effect worshipping the devil.

This is amazing, shocking and unbelievable, but true. God's word says it, and God's word is Truth. (John 17:17) John continues to write of America, the lamb-like beast, "...and he doeth great wonders so that he makes fire come down from heaven on the earth in the sight of men..." (Revelation 13:13)

Jesus Christ, when relating the events that would precede His Second Coming, predicted, "...There shall arise false Christs, and false prophets, and shall show great signs and wonders, insomuch that if it were possible, they shall deceive the very elect..." (Matthew 24:24)

Now, John declares that such miracles will take place in the period of America's leadership of the world as she forces men and women to worship the pope of Rome. To this end, these miracles are wrought. John explains, "...and deceives them that dwell on the earth by the means of those miracles which he had power to do in the sight of the first beast (the Papacy) saying to them that dwell on the earth, that they should make an image to the beast (first beast/Papacy) which had the wound by the sword and did live..." (Revelation 13:14).

The apostle Paul, in describing Jesus, expresses this thought, "...Who (Jesus) being the brightness of His (God the Father) glory, and the express image of His (God the Father) person..." (Hebrews 1:3). Jesus confirms, "...I and My Father are One...if you have seen Me you have seen the Father..." (John 10:30, John 14:9). Here, both Jesus Christ and the apostle Paul are making it very clear that Jesus is like unto His Father. He is the express image of His Father.

In similar fashion, John reports that the United States of America will become in character, exactly like the Papacy. That is what is meant by making an image to the (first) beast. (The Papacy)

And what is the Papacy? It is the amalgamation of pagan religious doctrines, sprinkled with enough Christianity to make it appear Christian. Those dogmas are then enforced and upheld by the power of the state under the influence of the church. That is the historic character of the Papacy. It is what the apostle John says that America will become.

America, the prophet foretells, will eventually move from its position of religious freedom and political openness, to one of religious intolerance and ruthless political and civil suppression. It will become exactly like the Papacy of old. In fact, it would be the Papacy, through her agents, that would skillfully bring this about.

Ellen G. White, the eloquent nineteenth century Christian writer, prophesies, "...By the decree enforcing the institution of the Papacy in violation of the law of God, our nation will disconnect herself fully from righteousness. When Protestantism shall stretch her hand across the gulf to grasp the hand of the Roman power, when she shall reach over the abyss to clasp hands with spiritualism, when under the influence of this threefold union, our country shall repudiate (abandon) every principle of it's Constitution as a Protestant and Republican government, and shall make provision for the propagation of papal falsehoods and delusions, then we may know that the time has come for the marvelous working of satan and that the end is near..." **(Testimonies for the Church,** Volume 5, page 451).

But America, John says, will do much more than become like the Papacy. He moves on, "...And he (America) had power to give life into the image of the beast, that the image of the beast should both speak, and cause that as many as would not worship the image of the beast should be killed..." (Revelation 13:15)

As the Papacy was described in the previous chapter as having worldwide power and influence so does America today. That power and influence coupled with a spirit of religious intolerance and political repression, will be developed into what John terms 'Image of the Beast'. In its position as the world's dominant military and police force; America will not only lead in legislating oppressive religious laws, but will force men around the world to obey those laws.

Disobedience to those worldwide decrees will result in imprisonment, deprivation and death. At the very core of that forced worship, John declares, will be the 'Mark of the Beast'. The point has already been made as to what is the Mark of the Beast, i.e. Sunday sacredness.

John's prophecy continues, "...And he (America) causes all, both small and great, rich and poor, free and bond, to receive a mark in their right hand, or in their foreheads...and that no man may buy or sell, save that he has the mark or the name of the beast, or the number of his name..." (Revelation 16:17)

Speculations abound about the matters of the mark, the image, the name and the number of the beast. But you need not be deceived. We have clearly established from historical records, Biblical prophecy and Papal decrees what is the beast and what is its mark. The mark is not a bar code nor a computer chip to be implanted in the forehead or right hand. It is not our computer. The mark is, as is emphatically stated and confirmed by the beast himself, Sunday sacredness. This is in contradiction to a free choice for God's blessed Sabbath-day.

According to John's prophecy, the United States will enact laws (speak) and enforce (cause) men everywhere to accept Sunday as a sacred day of worship in honor and recognition of the pope of Rome as the Vicar of Christ on the earth.

Providence aside, the resurgence, growth and eventual domination of America by the Papacy began in earnest with the election of Pope Pius X1 in 1922. In the classic, **Rome Stoops to Conquer,** by Jesuit scholar E. Boyd Barrett, we discover the following, "...Pius is well aware that the Catholic Church can never hope again to dominate the civilized world until America kneels, beaten and penitent at her feet…In teaching American Catholics this new phase of Catholicism, this active phase, and in sanctifying it with his blessings, Pius X1 rendered inevitable many significant changes in the life course of this nation…" (**Rome Stoops To Conquer**, pg 4)

The new phase here referred to was an aggressive, well defined and organized plan to control all aspects of American life. As we look around the American landscape today, no one can doubt that Pius' vision and initiatives to make America catholic have been resoundingly successful. Catholicism, through her dedicated sons and daughters, is in control of the media, business, government, the judiciary, politics and religion.

So successful is Rome's plan for America that we find the current president admonishing the nation to follow the teachings of the Roman Catholic church. He visited the Vatican to present to the late Pope John Paul II the Medal of Honor. This is the highest recognition our nation can give to an individual. What a pitiful sight it was to see three living American presidents paying homage to the Papacy by kneeling before the dead body of Pope John Paul II.

Pius' aim for America was and still is the centerpiece of the Vatican's strategy for world domination. Professor E. Boyd Bartlett continues, "…Though Pius has little liking for our wicked ways and our heresies, he sees in us the nation that counts for most in the world today- the nation of the future. We are rich, young, strong, and our life is before us as a nation… He would have us, he needs us; he means to have us. He believes that the destiny of the church will be fulfilled in America and that with the spiritual conquest of America, the world dominion of the church will be regained…" (**ibid** 259)

When Pius' vision for a Catholic America is fully manifested, then the church's mark of authority, Sunday sacredness, will be rigidly enforced.

But God has already given us a sacred day of rest. He gave it to us from creation. It is His holy and blessed Sabbath-day (Genesis 2:2,3). He has not changed it, nor has he given any man or organization the permission or authority to do so.

How then will men receive the Mark of the Beast? It is a choice one has to make. It is a decision that will determine your eternal destiny.

When this oppressive, worldwide decree is enacted and the evidence of God's true Sabbath is presented, as it is in this volume; then all will be required to make their choice either for God or for the devil. There is no middle ground. It is either God's Sabbath or the devil's Sunday. Everyone will have to choose either the seventh-day as ordained by God or the first day as instituted by man.

You receive the mark in your forehead when you reject the truth of God's Sabbath, and consciously choose to venerate Sunday in obedience to the Papacy. In the forehead is where the frontal lobe is housed. This is the part of the brain where we make decisions. By making a decision for Sunday, you would have declared to the universe that the devil and the pope of Rome are above the God of creation. You receive the mark on your right hand, when you say you believe the truth of God's Sabbath, but do not have enough faith to honor His command not to do any secular work on His Sabbath-day. By doing so, you demonstrate that you do not trust God sufficiently to provide for yourself and family. The matter is as simple, yet as profound as Eve choosing to eat the fruit that God commanded her not to eat.

Jesus beckons us, "…If you love me, keep my commandments…" (John 14:15). That includes the Sabbath commandment (Exodus 20:8 – 11). In the very words of God's commands lie the power to obey that which He commands. By faith you can and must obey.

The impending worldwide decree to enforce Sunday sacredness, with America as the chief enforcer, is not so far fetched at all.

Very soon after America's birth as a nation the spirit of Romanism began to raise its ugly head. Those who had fled religious persecution to find refuge in America attempted, with some success, to do exactly that which they ran away from.

For example, following the California gold rush of the 1840's, that state passed a law in 1859, forbidding business to open on Sunday. By 1882 more than 1600 violators were arrested. So heated was the issue of Sunday sacredness, that it found its way on the platform of both political parties in the general election of 1882.

In 1885 several persons were also arrested, jailed and/or fined in the state of Arkansas for violating that state's Sunday blue law, which prohibited work on Sunday. In 1889, both the state Supreme Court and U.S. Circuit Court upheld the conviction of a Tennessee man who violated that state's Sunday closing law.

Also, in 1889, the issue of Sunday sacredness was the substance of two bills introduced in the U.S. Senate by Senator H.W. Blair of New Hampshire. The first bill, calling for the promotion of Sunday as a national day of rest, referred to Sunday as "The Lord's Day." The other bill called for a constitutional amendment requiring the public schools to teach "the principle of the Christian Religion". That principle, as some perceived it, was honoring Sunday as the emblem of the nation's Christian identity. The same spirit is alive and well in the nation today.

Of course, those efforts failed to legislate a National Sunday Law. However, we are now at a point in the history of the United States, where a legislated National Day of Rest, (Sunday) is a real possibility. In fact, according to God's word, it is a sure reality. (Revelation 13:11-17)

As the nation experiences accelerating moral decay, unrelenting sexual promiscuity, increased violence and religious indifference, the calls are mounting to return to God by making Sunday a holy day. Organizations such as the Moral Majority, the Christian Coalition and the Lord's Day Alliance among others, are joining forces to force legislation for a national day of rest. These actions, well intentioned as they are, are not only a violation of our constitutional principles but an affront to the God of Creation.

They are verily a fulfillment of John's prophecy. God has given us His day of rest from creation. That day is His Holy Sabbath-day. (Genesis 2:2,3). He reminds us to keep it holy. (Exodus 20:8-11). He has sent His prophets to teach us about it, and has given Jesus Christ as our example to honor it.

Yet men have cast it aside. They are attempting to establish their own standard of righteousness by elevating Sunday to the place of God's Sabbath. Jesus warned the religious leaders of His day, "…This people honor Me with their lips, but their heart is far from Me...Howbeit in vain do they worship Me, teaching for doctrines the commandments of men...for laying aside the commandment of God, ye hold the tradition of men..." (Mark 7:6-8).

With regards to God's Sabbath, this is exactly what men and women, professing to be Christians, are doing in the exhalation of Sunday. Jesus asks,"...And why call ye Me Lord, Lord, and do not the things which I say? (Luke 6:46)

America is a nation that is abundantly blessed with God's bounties, including an overflowing of His word. Too many people, claiming to belong to Him, are unfortunately choosing not only to worship the devil, but also are seeking to force the whole nation to do likewise. This is deception of the highest order.

Paul addresses the issue, "...Because that, when they know God, they glorified Him not as God, neither were thankful; but became vain in their imaginations, and their foolish heart was darkened...professing themselves to be wise, they became fools..." (Romans 1:21,22) He continues, "...And with all deceivableness of unrighteousness in them that perish; because they received not the love of the truth, that they might be saved... and for this cause God shall send them strong delusions that they should believe a lie: that they all might be damned, who believe not the truth, but had pleasure in unrighteousness..." (2 Thessalonians 2:10-12)

How sad for a people who have been given so much by Almighty God. As America continues her march toward tearing down God's holy law, whilst uplifting the traditions of the man of sin in its place, great tribulation and destruction will befall the nation along with the rest of the world. As the nation, under the pretense of greater security, repudiates the principles of its constitution, it will be swept swiftly under total control of Romanism and horrible cruelties will follow.

Some, however, will be faithful to the God of creation. Even in such a time as these, God's character will be vindicated by those, who in the face of deprivation and death, will uphold His holy Sabbath-day. This has always been the history of God's people. Like Luther, like Elijah, like Shadrach, Meshach and Abednego and multitudes of others,

God' true disciples will stand, even unto death, in this imminent crisis. The question is, will you be one of them?

In our next chapter, we will further examine America, the Papacy and the signs of the times. We will discover that God's Sabbath is indeed the test of these times. Understanding God's Sabbath is truly the knowledge that God's people should seek.

CHAPTER 9
The Sabbath and The Signs of The Times

Perhaps the most revealing book on world affairs in the last decade is the volume '**Keys Of This Blood**' by Malachi Martin. Malachi Martin, now deceased, was a Roman Catholic Jesuit priest. He was also a history scholar with immense insight into the plans and purposes of the Papacy and her relations with America and the world at large.

In this eye opening account of the Papacy's plans for world domination, Martin writes, "...Willing or not, ready or not, we are all involved in an all-out, no-holds-barred three way global competition. Most of us are not competitors, however, we are the stakes. For the competition is about who will establish the first one-world system of government that had ever existed in the society of nations. It is about who will hold and wield the dual power and authority and control over each of us as individuals and over all of us as a community; over the entire six billion people expected by demographers to inhabit the earth by early in the 3rd millennium..."

Malachi Martin continues, "...The competition is all out because, now that it has been started, there is no way it can be reversed or called off. No-holds-barred because, once the competition has been decided, the world and all that's in it – our way of life as individuals and as citizens of the nations; our families and our jobs; our trade and commerce and money; our educational systems and our religions and our cultures; even the badges of our national identity, which most of us have already taken for granted – all will have been powerfully and radically altered forever. No one can be exempted from its effects. No sector of our lives will remain untouched…"

The Jesuit professor elaborates, "…The competition began and continues as a three-way affair because that is the number of rivals with sufficient resources to establish and maintain a New World Order. Nobody who is acquainted with the plans of these three rivals has any doubt but that only one of them can win. Each expects the other two to be overwhelmed and swallowed up in the coming maelstrom of change…"

He concludes, "…That being the case, it would appear inescapable that their competition will end up in confrontation. It is not too much to say in fact, that the chosen purpose of John Paul's Pontificate, the engine that drives his papal grand policy and that determines his day- to- day, year- to- year strategies is to be the victor in that competition, well underway…" (**Keys of this Blood**, page 15)

In addition to the Papacy, Malachi Martin goes on to identify the other two competitors as Communism, exemplified by the Soviet Union and Globalism, exemplified by western capitalist nations with America at the helm. One can easily ascertain that both Communism and Globalism are political/military entities. They are therefore obvious contenders in this competition. But the church of Rome; how does it get into the mix of geopolitical intrigue, and where is its military and geopolitical might?

Avro Manhattan answers those questions in his book, **Vatican Imperialism in the 20th Century**. He writes, "…Although without armies, navies and super hydrogen bombs, the Vatican has more power at its disposal than if it had the greatest military capability. The pope's government is as important as that of the USA, of Russia or of China except territorially and spiritually, it is far larger and it exerts more influence than the three combined…"

Encyclopedia Americana describes Catholicism thus, "…The Papacy is the oldest continuing absolute monarchy in the world. To millions, the pope is the infallible interpreter of divine revelation and the Vicar of Christ; to others he is the fulfillment of the Biblical prophecies about the coming of the antichrist…"

It goes on to state, "…Thus the Roman Catholic Church is

itself a complex institution, for which the usual diagram of a pyramid, extending from the pope at the apex to the believers in the pew, is vastly oversimplified. Within that institution, moreover, sacred congregations, archdioceses and dioceses, provinces, religious orders and societies, seminaries and colleges, parishes and confraternities, and countless other institutions all invite the social scientist to the consideration of power relations, leadership roles, social dynamics, and other sociological connections that it uniquely represents..."

That most reputable resource concludes, "...As a world religion among world religions, Roman Catholicism in its belief and practice manifests, somewhere within the range of its multicolored life, some of the features of every religion of the human race; thus only the methodology of comparative religion can encompass them all..."

Of the Papacy's wealth, Avro Manhattan, a world recognized authority on the Roman Catholic Church writes, "...The Vatican's treasure of solid gold has been estimated by the United Nations World Magazine, to amount to several billion dollars. A large bulk of this is stored with the United States Federal Reserve Bank, while banks in England and Switzerland hold the rest. But this is just a small portion of the wealth of the Vatican, which in the U.S. alone is greater than that of the five wealthiest giant corporations of this country. When to that is added all the real estate property, stocks and shares abroad, then the staggering accumulation of the wealth of the Catholic Church becomes so formidable as to defy any rational assessment..." (**Vatican Billions**)

The above descriptions, without any reference to spiritual things, are in total and complete agreement with the Biblical account of this power.

John the Revelator writes, "...And the woman was arrayed in purple and scarlet color, and decked with gold and precious stones and pearls, having a golden cup in her hand full of abominations and filthiness of her fornication: and upon her forehead was a name written, Mystery Babylon The Great, the Mother of Harlots and abominations of the Earth..." (Revelation 17:4-5). "...And the beast which I saw was like unto a leopard, and his feet were as the feet of a bear, and his mouth of a lion: and the dragon gave him his power, and his seat and great authority..." (Revelation 13:2)

These Scriptural references to a religious organization which encompasses many religious practices and is exceedingly wealthy, undoubtedly point to the Roman Catholic Church. Coupled with the historical facts presented in earlier chapters, the evidence becomes compelling and the identification clearer.

With the foregoing descriptions, both from the Biblical and secular perspectives, the Papacy legitimately earns its position as one of the three contenders for world domination. Malachi Martin, perhaps not referring to the Biblical account, which he coincidently agrees with, is correct in his conclusion that the Papacy will become the victor in the world's three way competition for world domination.

All major governments of the world are, to a great extent, under the influence and control of the Papacy. This is possible through her sons and daughters who have worked themselves up to the highest positions of power and influence within those governments. As these individuals make decisions, they make them not with the interests of their individual country in mind; but ultimately their decisions are in accordance with the aims and in the best interest of the Papacy. As devout Roman Catholics, their allegiance is first and foremost to their church and not to the countries in which they live.

As members of the Papacy's several secret organizations, fraternities and societies, these individuals are sworn to uphold and advance the aims of the Papacy. That overwhelming aim, as Malachi Martin points out, is to regain full and undisputed control of the world and make every human being on planet earth a servant of the pope of Rome.

Thus we read, "... When the Pope is crowned, he is reminded that he is the father of princes, and kings, and the supreme judge of the universe, and on earth, the vicar of Jesus Christ our Savior, and the governor of the world..." (Lucius Ferrais, **Ecclesiastical Dictionary**, 1793). The boast is re-emphasized, "...We define that the Holy Apostolic Sea and the Roman Pontiff holds the primacy over the whole world..." (**The Most Holy Councils,** Vol. 13, col. 1167, Phillippe

Labbe and Gabriela Cossant).

Rome's objective is clear; i.e. to become the undisputed religious and political ruler of the entire world. Let's now consider the positions and roles of the other two contenders in Malachi Martin's account of contemporary world affairs.

On February 24, 1992, **Time Magazine's** cover headline read, "...HOLY ALLIANCE. How Reagan and the pope conspired to assist Poland's solidarity movement and hasten the demise of Communism..." As the sub-line indicates, the Papacy headed by Pope John Paul II, and the Globalists headed by the United States of America with Ronald Reagan as president, joined forces to neutralize or otherwise defeat Soviet Communism.

The article went on to state, "...The key administration players were all Roman Catholics – CIA Chief William Casey, Allen, Clarke, Haig, Walters and William Wilson, Reagan's first ambassador to the Vatican. They regarded the U.S./Vatican relationship as a Holy Alliance: the moral force of the pope and the teachings of their church combined with their fierce anti-communism and their notion of American democracy. Yet the mission would have been impossible without the full support of Reagan, who believed fervently in both the benefits and the practical applications of Washington's relationship with the Vatican. One of the earliest goals as President, Reagan says, was to recognize the Vatican as a state and make them an ally..." (**ibid,** pg. 31)

President Reagan had made good on his promise to recognize the Vatican as a state and making it an ally. He subsequently appointed William Wilson as the first US ambassador to the Vatican. Wilson is a devout Roman Catholic and an alleged member of the secret papal society, the Knights of Malta. No other religious organization enjoys that privilege. In fact, most nations also have ambassadors to the Vatican. This a phenomenon unheard of in any other religious body.

The article continues, "...Nobody believed the collapse of communism would happen this fast on the time table... says a cardinal who is one of the pope's closest aides. But in their first meeting, the Holy Father and the President committed themselves and the institutions of the church and America to such a goal. And from that day, the focus was to bring it about in Poland… " (**ibid**, pg. 35)

Of the meeting between President Reagan and Pope John Paul II, **Time** also reported, "…On June 7, 1982, Reagan and John Paul met for fifty minutes at the Vatican. During that conversation, the plot was hatched to eliminate communism. In that meeting, Reagan and the Pope agreed to undertake a clandestine campaign to hasten the dissolution of the communist regime. Declares Richard Allen, Reagan's first National Security adviser… This was one of the great secret alliances of all time…" (**ibid**, pg. 28)

Today, we all know the result of that 'Holy Alliance'. The Berlin wall has fallen and Germany is united into one nation. The Soviet Union has collapsed and its economy is in shambles. It's military might reduced to a barking dog without teeth.

Now, there are two remaining in the competition for the New World Order and world domination. The United States of America as she leads the world's Globalists, and Catholicism with its velvet glove of religion masking its iron hand of worldwide military and political capacity.

Though their objectives are the same, each is employing a different strategy. The Papacy is leading out with its religion. America prides herself on her military might and considers that to be her most effective weapon in creating a world empire. To a great extent, many on the Globalists' side are either unaware, willingly ignorant or are in denial of the Papacy's position as a major contender for establishing the New World Order. But make no mistake, Rome's agents within the Globalists' camp are not only aware of the Vatican's objectives, but rather are working assiduously to achieve it.

As the late Pope John Paul II traveled to every corner of the globe, he preached a gospel of peace, unity and co-existence for all mankind. The Papacy has systematically continued on it's path of bringing all religions together into one great world religion, with the pope as its sole, authoritative leader. Major protestant religions have bought into this scheme. The Lutherans, the Anglicans along with other major Christian movements have accepted the pope as the divine primate of the Christian church. Evangelical leaders such as Billy

Graham, Chuck Colson, Pat Robertson, Robert Schuler and others are calling for unity and cooperation with the Papacy.

Billy Graham takes the lead by proclaiming, "...He (John Paul II) has brought the greatest impact of any Pope. I admire his courage, determination, and intellectual abilities and his understanding of Catholic, Protestant and Orthodox differences and the attempt at some form of reconciliation..." (**Associated Press**)

This sort of sentiment is in perfect harmony with Rome's strategy to bring all religions under the primacy of the pope of Rome.

We find this declaration in the Roman Catholic Publication, **The Struggle of World Catholicism**, pg. 28, " ...The World Council of Churches, in its implementation of the Vatican II Strategy of creating a universal celebration service to focus the conscience in harmony with the sacred and certain teaching of the Catholic Church, sees as absolutely crucial and indispensable, continuation of the liturgical celebration in all dimensions of life. Clearly, liturgical celebration is conceived as being the molder and shaper, the conditioner, of all dimensions of human life. This is all very interesting in light of Rome's policy of Integralism. Integralism means that all human life would be integrated, as John Paul II conceives, into a 'perfect society' in which laity works under the direction of priests and bishops to achieve the 'truth' of a life lived in faith..."

In plain language, every human being will be brought under the undisputed control of Rome as each one renders cadaver obedience to her priests. This is in keeping with the Catholic church's historical character.

Following the Papacy's blueprint and long-term strategy for world domination, the pope of Rome has made his pilgrimage to all major religions. He has solicited and gained their support and favor for a One World Religion in the name of world peace and universal unity. Thus we found John Paul II bowing down before the throne of Buddhism's chief monk. He has taken the mark of the god Shiva from a Hindu high priestess.

In his travels, Pope John Paul found comfort and commonality in praying with the leaders of Buddhism, Hinduism, Islam, Judaism,

African tribal witch doctors, Asian Shamans, Zoroastrian fire worshippers and Togo snake handlers. He declared that none of these need to accept Jesus to be saved. Salvation, the church declares, can only be found within the confines of Roman Catholicism. Of those that believe in Jesus, the Papacy insists that they should honor the day of the sun rather than God's blessed Sabbath-day.

The Scripture, however, declares in Jesus's words, "... I Am the way the Truth and the Life; no one cometh unto the Father but by Me..." (John 14:6). Jesus' way to honor His Father, is by commemorating God's holy Sabbath-day, the seventh day of the week, today called Saturday.

It is irrelevant to the Papacy what your religion is, provided that it is not the Creator's religion. God's religion is the religion that upholds the seventh-day Sabbath and teaches that faith in Jesus Christ is your only salvation from sin.

Catholicism is fiercely antagonistic to the true religion of the God of creation. But Catholicism is unapologetically accommodating, rather, consisting of the rites, rituals, ceremonies, practices and beliefs of all false and pagan religions.

Their common bond lies in the belief of the natural immortality of the soul and their adoration of the sun. These are the ties that bind them together and the glue that provides for a one-world religion.

John prophesies, "... and his (the Papacy) deadly wound was healed and all the world wondered after the beast... and they worshipped the dragon which gave power unto the beast and they worshipped the beast, saying, who is able to make war with him... and all that dwell upon the earth shall worship him (the Papacy) whose names are not written in the book of life of the Lamb slain from the foundation of the world..." (Revelation 13:3, 4, 8)

In all this, Rome's total and unquestioned domination of the world is not quite complete. There is but one hurdle standing in her way. If she can eliminate this one obstacle, then her goal of unchallenged world domination, with forced Sunday worship will be achieved. That obstacle is the Constitution of the United States of America.

Though united with America in the demise of Communism, the

Papacy yet harbors a deep-rooted disdain and hatred for the American Constitution and its precepts of civil and religious liberties.

Richard W. Thompson, Secretary of the Navy during the Lincoln years writes in his book, **The Papacy and Civil Power**: "...Nothing is plainer than that. If the principles of the Church of Rome prevail here, our Constitution would necessarily fail. The two cannot exist together. They are in open and direct antagonism with the fundamental history of our government and of all popular governments everywhere..."

The Papacy plays both ends of the fiddle for its own self interest. This is her strategy relative to the United States of America In her quest for control of the New World Order

The church of Rome confirms, "...If Catholics ever gain a sufficient numerical majority in this country, religious freedom is at an end. So our enemies say, so we believe..." (**The Shepherd of the Valley**, Official Journal of the Bishop of St. Louis, November 23, 1851).

Pope Pius IX declared in 1854, "...The absurd and erroneous doctrines and ravening in defense of liberty are a most pestilential error, a pest of all other, most to be dreaded..." Pope Gregory XVI agreed, "...Liberty of conscience is a mad opinion..." The U.S. Constitution, which guarantees the freedom of worship, freedom of the press and all other freedoms, is deemed by pope Gregory XVI to be, "...a filthy sewer filled with heretical vomit..."

Since the Papacy holds fast to the claim of papal infallibility, then it must be concluded that these statements still represent Rome's policy towards the United States of America.

Such is Rome's hatred of the United States Constitution. Ellen G. White in her inspiring work, **The Great Controversy**, declares, "...The Roman Church now presents a fair front to the world, covering with apologies her record of horrible cruelties. She has clothed herself in Christ like garments, but she is unchanged. Every principle of the Papacy that existed in past ages exists today. The doctrines devised in the dark ages are still held..." (page 571)

So wily, cunning and deceptive is the Roman power, that the very one she cooperated with to eliminate Communism, is the one she

seeks to conquer and use as her instrument, in achieving her perceived role as ruler of the whole earth. This was exactly her strategy during the Dark Ages when the Roman
Church ruled supreme.

She used a weakened and divided imperial power to enforce her doctrines and dogmas.

With her universal rule, comes her anti-Christian dogmas and doctrines. As the ruler of this one-world religious order and one-world system of government, the pope of Rome has no fear or doubt that his church will control the consciences of men everywhere and persecute, even unto death those who will not submit to her rule.

The deceived, ever widening, influential ecumenical movement guarantees the ultimate dictatorship of the Papacy over every person on planet earth. With the power and might of America at her disposal, Romanism will once again manifest the same spirit of tyranny and oppression as she did during the Dark Ages.

H.G. Wells observed in his book, **Crux Ansata**: "…Roman Catholicism presents many faces to the world, but everywhere it is systematic in its fight against freedom…."

And so it is in America today. Whilst publicly proclaiming to promote liberty, the agents of Rome are the very ones working, yea stealthily but aggressively, to destroy that which they openly pretend to defend.

The Catholic Research information Bureau, a British watchdog group that tracks the moves of the Papacy, sounds this strong and sober warning, "…Don't be deceived. The Roman Catholic Church is like a chameleon; tolerant, friendly, highly moral and authoritative in Protestant England and America, but where there is a Roman Catholic majority, she is very different and no friend of freedom, always blending in with the landscape,
but never quite what she seems to be…"

Whilst America, the last remaining military and economic superpower, projects the image of might and force to accomplish her goal of world domination, Catholicism is working aggressively, yet stealthily, even within the American power structure, to destroy

America's Constitution, weaken America economically, then rise to use America's might to dominate
America and the rest of the world.

Catholicism, through her appointed agents, is orchestrating the chaos and demise of world governments. She will then rise, like a phoenix from the ashes of that ruin, to be hailed as the savior of mankind. As the Roman Church rose to power and prominence out of the chaos of a disintegrating Roman Empire, so will it rise out of the fear and confusion of a chaotic world, presenting itself as the world's only hope for survival.

The Papacy is able to accomplish this through her agents. They are the members of her several secret organizations such as the Jesuits, Opus Dei, the Knights of Columbus, the Knights of Malta, and other powerful and influential elements within the power structure of the American government and other governments worldwide. These agents hold the keys of power and influence in the American government, businesses, education, media, religion, the judicial system and every other facet of life. Their aim is singular, i.e. to restore Catholicism to the governorship of the world, by whatever means necessary.

Their loyalty to the pope of Rome outweighs, in great measure, their respect for the American Constitution or the rule of law of any government. Their decisions and policies are not to advance freedom and the American way of life, but rather to reestablish Rome as the winner in the global competition for world domination.

In her effort, Rome is aided by the deceived political and religious leaders who know not the true aims of the Papacy. Dr. John W. Robbins, a leading authority on Roman Catholicism makes this eye opening assertion, "…The Roman church/state is a hybrid, a monster of ecclesiastical and political power. Its political thought is totalitarian and whenever it has had the opportunity to apply its principles, the result has been bloody repression. If during the last 30 years it has softened its assertions of full, supreme and irresponsible power and has murdered fewer people than before; such changes of behavior are not due to a change in its ideas but to a change in circumstances… it is only when the Roman church/state faced public opinion that disapproved of church/state sanctioned murder, that it slowed its persecutions and attempted to speak with a voice less bloodthirsty. The Roman church/state in the 20th century, however, is an institution recovering from a deadly wound. If and when it regains it's full power and authority, it will impose a regime more sinister than any the planet has ever seen..." (**Ecclesiastical Megalomania,** Dr. John W. Robbins)

Former Chief Justice William Rehnquist declared, "...The wall of separation between church and state is a metaphor based on bad history, a metaphor which has proved useless as a guide to judging. It should be frankly and explicitly abandoned..."

Tim LaHaye, a popular, self-proclaimed Christian writer states, "...The only hope for revival in America is (religious) legislative reform..."

Pat Robertson, founder of the Christian Coalition is quite emphatic when he declared, "...We are working shoulder to shoulder with Roman Catholics and other people of faith..."

Keith Fournier, Executive Director of the American Center for Law and Justice and leading Roman Catholic, exclaimed, "...The wall of separation between church and state that was erected by secular humanists and other enemies of religious freedom has to come down. That wall is more of a threat to society than the Berlin wall ever was..."

These notions, though good sounding on the surface, are all injurious to the American way of life. They are antagonistic to, and subversive of the American Constitution. They are the outworkings of the Vatican's plan to take over America and the world.

With America's help, knowingly and willingly,(Catholicism) the beast from the sea demolished the Berlin wall. With America's help, ignorantly but willingly, the beast is destroying that wall of separation between church and state and whatever is left of the American Constitution. She has vastly demolished the wall of separation between Protestantism and Catholicism.

The U.S. House of Representatives, in the year 2000 voted 416-1 in favor of increased Vatican influence in the United Nations. In a measure brought before the Congress involving U.S. Policy towards abortion, Representative Dick Armey of Texas a proclaimed, "...The

Vatican is under attack by pro-abortion extremists, and Congress will not tolerate this effort to silence the Vatican..." Representative Christopher H. Smith of New Jersey agreed, but pushed the idea a bit further. Said he, "...If anything, the Holy See deserves a more prominent role in the UN..." They are both prominent Roman Catholics.

Most frightening however, is what President George Bush proclaimed, on the eve of the dedication ceremony of a monument in the nation's capital, in honor of pope John Paul II. Surrounded by the Catholic elite in America, the president declared, "...The best way to honor Pope John Paul II, truly one of the great men, is to take his teaching seriously... to listen to his words and put his words and teachings into action here in America. This is a challenge we must accept..."

It is quite disturbing to hear the president of the United States of America express such sentiments. It truly epitomizes the mis-education of the American people, including the current president. America is the last bastion of civil and religious freedoms in the world. The United States of America is a country that was born out of resistance to papal persecution. The founding fathers passionately embraced the ideas of the Protestant Reformation. Today, however, America is certainly beginning to speak like the prophetic dragon (Revelation 13:11).

Every citizen should be much alarmed to hear the president encourage the nation to worship the pope of Rome, thus rejecting the God of creation. It is impossible to follow the teachings of Roman Catholicism and truly serve the God of creation at the same time. The traditions of Rome are in open contradiction to the word of God and the precepts of the American way of life. We have shown several examples of this as it relates to freedom of worship and liberty of conscience. The two are diametrically opposed to each other. The ideals of Americanism and the practices of popery are mutually irreconcilable concepts.

Nevertheless, a call for unity with Rome by America's political and religious leaders is exactly what is proclaimed in this race for world domination. The end result is inescapable. Rome will triumph and

America will submit. That's what God's word says. (Revelation 13:11-17). Malachi Martin, though not speaking the oracles of God, arrives at the same conclusion in his book Keys to this Blood.

Since his election as president, George Bush has consistently sought the advice of leading Roman Catholic Bishops and other prominent Roman Catholic thought leaders, in formulating both his domestic and foreign policies. The president is famous for his regular breakfast meetings with the leading Roman Catholic clergy in the United States. No other religious body enjoys that privilege.

Today, the Congress of the United States is more than 40% Catholic. The Supreme Court is a majority Catholic with a Roman Catholic Chief Justice. For the very first time in U.S. history, the country is being lead spiritually, via the U.S. House of representatives, by a Roman Catholic Chaplain. We have a Roman Catholic Attorney General.

These are not mere coincidences. They are rather, a skillfully orchestrated, carefully executed campaign to make America Catholic. They are the outworking Pius XI campaign to take over America.

Richard John Nehaus, formerly a Lutheran minister, but now a convert to Catholicism, remarked in his address to the Catholic Campaign for America conference, "…We Catholics belong in America in order to change the way things have been done in America for so long. Catholics have a distinct responsibility because of their size and mission. The bride of Christ is not for hire. We cannot be bound by other coalitions. There would be no pro-life movement were it not for Catholic Americans. The great question is truth – moral truth. Truth is determined by the majority as we are told by John Paul II in his encyclical, Contisensus Annus …"

God disagrees. God says that His word is truth. (John 17:17). God determines what is truth for man. No man can make that determination for other men. God says that His Commandments are truth. (Psalms 119: 142)

It must be noted here, that most Catholics, like the rest of society, have no idea as to what their church is all about. Nowhere in our discussion in this volume are we referring to the millions of God fearing, peace loving people who find themselves the unwitting victims of this massive system of deceit and deception. We are discussing a hierarchy, whose only mission is to reestablish Roman Catholicism, with its doctrine of submit or die, at the apex of all humanity.

September 11, 2001 has brought us to a new era in the war for world domination. The attack on the World Trade Center and the Pentagon signaled the beginning of fresh onslaughts on the American Constitution. Following the so-called terrorists' attacks, the country has experienced the passage of the Patriot Act I & II, the enactment of the Homeland Security Act and Presidential Executive Order implementing Faith Based Initiative. All these measures, along with other Presidential initiatives, curtailing civil liberties, have accelerated the march towards destruction of the sacred ark of the people's covenant.

With all attention focused and blame heaped on Islamic terrorists and the worldwide campaign of fear, few are paying much attention to the attack on the American Constitution. The question begs to be answered? 'who benefits from such destruction of the Constitution?'

Unquestionably, that precious depository of American happiness is being devalued and desecrated. This sacred instrument which allows us to enjoy the freedoms we do as a nation, is being torn apart in the name of security. Ever so subtlety, but rather presumptuously, the Constitution is being torn down, ostensibly for security of the nation in a time of war.

It would perhaps be helpful for those who insist that a curtailment of our constitutional rights is justified to increase security, to refocus on the following, "...The Constitution of the United States is a law for rulers and people, equally in war and in peace, and covers with the shield of its protection all classes of men, at all times, and under all circumstances. No doctrine, involving more pernicious consequences, was ever invented by the wit of man than that any of its provisions can be suspended during any of the great exigencies of government. Such a doctrine leads directly to anarchy or despotism, for the theory of necessity on which it is based is false; for the government, within the Constitution, has all the power granted to it, which are necessary to preserve its existence..." (Excerpt from Supreme Court opinion rendered at the time of the Civil War. Ex Parte Milligan, 71 US 2 (1866).

The Supreme Court must have been echoing the sentiments of Benjamin Franklin when those words were penned. Says the respected founding father, "...Those who would give up essential liberty to purchase a little temporary safety deserve neither liberty nor safety..."

The Patriot Acts, Homeland Security and numerous other Presidential initiatives since September 11, 2001, serve only to deprive Americans of their God given, constitutionally confirmed, civil and religious liberties. It does not, as the agents of Rome and deceived Americans believe, increase the security of the nation.

The security of the American people is not the goal of the agents of Rome who control the horns of power in American society. Their goal is to bring America to her knees and establish the pope of Rome as leader of the New World Order.

As we have earlier pointed out, the Papacy, the beast coming out of the sea, (Revelation 13:1) will once again rule the world (Revelation 13:4,8). We have also discovered that the beast coming out of the earth, America (Revelation 13:11), would not only support the Papacy in its effort to regain control of the world; but, would itself become like the Papacy, an intolerant, persecuting power.

America is swiftly fulfilling her prophetic role in becoming the image of the beast. (Revelation 13:11-17) We have revealed what Scripture says about the mark of the beast. That mark we discovered is Sunday sacredness.

Further, we discovered that America will not only become like the Papacy, a persecuting religious autocracy; but that it will in fact enforce the religious dogmas and doctrines of the Papacy, primarily the mark of Rome's authority, Sunday sacredness. (Revelation 13:12-17). We have positively shown that Sunday sacredness is in direct and open opposition to God's holy Sabbath-day.

Clearly, we are heading into a period of great distress and unrest on a scale never before witnessed by human eyes. We are witnessing unrest in the Middle east, tribal conflicts in Africa, political instability in South America and other parts of the world, worldwide terrorism, AIDS, SARS and other epidemics, tsunamis and hurricanes of unprecedented magnitudes, pestilences and a universal campaign of fear, the effect of which will be international chaos and confusion. All these phenomenon is converging into a moment of unimaginable and unmanageable chaos and confusion. It will be a time when the whole world will be looking and calling for a savior.

At that time, all men will turn to religion as a cure for their dilemma. Who will your savior be? Would it be the pope of Rome and Sunday sacredness, or Jesus Christ and His blessed Sabbath-day? All will have to choose one or the other.

That is the most important issue for those who claim the name of Christ. There will be no middle ground. God in his mercy is allowing all alive to choose Him. John reports, "...And I saw another angel ascending from the east, having the seal of the living God: and he cried with a loud voice to the four angels, to whom it was given to hurt the earth and the sea... saying, Hurt not the earth, neither the sea, nor the trees, till we have sealed the servants of God in their foreheads..." (Revelation 7:2, 3). He continues, "...And I saw another angel fly in the midst of heaven having the everlasting gospel to preach unto them that dwell on the earth and to every nation and kindred and tongue and people, saying with a loud voice, fear God and give glory to him: for the hour of His judgment is come, and worship Him that made heaven, and earth, and the sea and the fountains of water..." (Revelation 14:6,7). John appeals to God's people, "...Come out of her, my people, that ye be not partakers of her sins, and that ye receive not of her plagues..." (Revelation 18:4).

This is a recurring call to reject religious confusion, headed by the Papacy and promulgated by her deceived daughters. God is calling His people to come into a sincere, obedient relationship with Him, the God of creation and Lord of the Sabbath.

God the Creator is yet calling men and women to worship Him in truth and righteousness by honoring His seventh-day Sabbath. The antichrist through the papal power, is calling for ecumenical unity and worship of a man and his mark, i.e. the pope of Rome and Sunday sacredness. Whom will you choose?

As a Christian, you must choose God. That means honoring His blessed Sabbath-day. You must make your decision soon. America is well on her way to transforming herself into the image of the beast. The United States of America will become acutely similar to Roman Catholicism of the Dark Ages. Not only will the U.S take on the persona of popery, but she will support it in the enforcement of its mark, Sunday sacredness.

Malachi Martin was right. The Papacy will become the victor in the competition for global domination. Not becausem he (Malachi Martin) or the Papacy says so, but because God prophesied it so.

Only in choosing the God of creation, will you be able to withstand the unmitigated fury of the beast (Roman Catholicism) and her image (The United States of America), as they compel the world to worship the pope of Rome by the
observance of Sunday in the place of the Lord's holy Sabbath-day.

In the next chapter, we will discover the dilemma in which Christians find themselves as they seek unity with the papal power. It is a dilemma that compels them to make a concerted decision with respect to God's holy Sabbath -day.

CHAPTER 10

The Sabbath and The Ecumenical Movement

Dilemma. Discovery. Decision.

Sometime in the year 1994, a landmark document was completed and signed by leading Roman Catholics and prominent Evangelical 'Protestants'. It was well publicized both in the secular and religious media. The initiative was hailed across denominational lines as a new beginning of cooperation between Catholics and Protestants.

The document, entitled Evangelicals and Catholics Together (ECT), sought to bring together the many Christian factions into one communion of the body of Christ under the aegis of the church of Rome.

The very thought that such a document could be conceived a few decades ago is incomprehensible. Oh, but how far have we come. Who would have imagined that such a proposition would not only be possible; but would be endorsed by a wide cross section of Christian leaders and accepted by multitudes of Christians.

From a Biblical perspective, one would only have to read and understand the 13th and 17th chapters of the book of Revelation to grasp the significance of such a development. Scripture foretells that such attempts at unity between Roman Catholics and professed Christians would take place on the threshold of Jesus' imminent return. According to Scripture, this conglomeration will not be for the good of society, but for the persecution of God's true followers. (Revelation 17:12-14).

In defining the unity which this document seeks to achieve, the Roman Catholic Apostle's Creed was quoted. This creed recites the belief of all adherents to the efficacy of the Roman Catholic Church as the only means of salvation for all believers.

All who sign this document, therefore, subscribe to this belief. Herein lies the great problem for this writer and others who seek salvation through the only One who can give it, Jesus Christ. This is a grave dilemma in which Bible-believing Christians, who support this and other similar accords, find themselves.

The Scriptures are abundantly clear. Our Savior declares, "… I am the Way, the Truth and the Life. No one cometh unto the Father but by Me…" (John 14:6). The apostle Peter, no doubt believing what his Savior had taught, exclaimed to his Jewish brethren, "…Neither is there salvation in any other; for there is none other name under heaven given among men whereby we must be saved…." (Acts 4:12).

The ECT document is a masterpiece of Roman Catholic propaganda. Other than being led by God's Holy Spirit, to whom ironically the ECT document also appeals, one could barely discern the truth mingled with tradition and outright error. The signatories to the ECT document consistently call for unity among Catholics and Protestants in the name of Jesus Christ. This is a grave deception.

The prophet Amos asks us, "…Can two walk together except they agree…" (Amos 3:3). The apostle Paul admonishes Christian believers, "…Be ye not unequally yoked with unbelievers. For what fellowship hath righteousness with unrighteousness and what communion hath light with darkness…" (2 Corinthians 6:14). How then can this document or any attempt at unity between Roman Catholicism and Protestantism be the will of God, as the ECT document claims?

Catholicism by its very nature, teachings and doctrines is contrary to the Christian faith. Whatever common ground it finds with Christianity is not patently Christian at all. Rather, commonality can only be found in some basic moral values professed by almost all mankind, religious and non-religious alike. This is indeed a good thing. It is upon this notion that the ECT and other Roman Catholic initiatives at 'church' unity are built. But here ends the similarity between Christianity and Catholicism. Beyond these core human values,

Catholicism differs from Christianity as night differs from day. These were the differences that gave rise to Protestantism.

Protestantism grew out of the belief that men and women are to seek God and salvation according to the dictates of their own consciences, and not the dogmas of the Catholic church. Hence the word, 'Protestants'. They were protesting against the unbiblical teachings of the 'church,' none of which have been renounced by her.

As we look across the religious landscape today and peruse documents like ECT, one is forced to ask the question, where are the Protestants? Who would have believed that the Lutheran church, founded by the most famous Protestant Reformer, Martin Luther, would find its way back to Rome?

The idea of Protestantism was born in that period of earth's history termed the Dark Ages. It was thus called because the Roman Catholic church, as she ruled the world, (538AD-1798AD) made it her first order of business to keep the word of God away from the people. God 's word teaches, "...Thy word is a lamp unto my feet and a light unto my path..." (Psalms 119:165). Since the Word was taken away, then there was only darkness left. Hence the term 'Dark Ages'.

In the place of God's word was substituted a plethora of pagan doctrines, church traditions and ecclesiastical dogmas. Although many of them continue today with Christian names and connotations, their essential falsity still remains. A prime example is Sunday sacredness which was instituted in the place of God's holy Sabbath-day.

Could Martin Luther and the other Protestant Reformers see from their graves, they would be appalled at how the nations, led by America, are clamoring back to Rome. They would be mystified at how, in a day when the Bible is freely and readily available, men are turning from the light of God's word to the darkness of Rome's traditions.

Times seem to be changing, however. The same Evangelicals who so readily seek unity with the Romish church, are now calling for the return of the nations to God's Ten Commandments law. It is a glorious discovery on their part. Particularly in light of the fact that almost all of them have vigorously taught that God's law was nailed to the cross at the crucifixion of Jesus Christ and therefore we do not have to keep them. The Seventh-day Adventists, building their faith on the Bible alone, have always taught and practiced that God's moral law is binding upon all men for all times.

It is quite puzzling, yet comforting, to see the great interest expressed by the Evangelicals for the display of the Ten Commandments in the public square. It is also not only ironic, but woefully laughable, considering the fact that the very vocal proponents, movers and shakers of this phenomenon are the very ones that have traditionally taught that the law of God was done away with at Calvary. They loudly proclaimed, rather confidently, that we are not under law but under grace and therefore do not have to keep the law. They parroted that the law was only for the Jews. For those, like the Seventh-day Adventists, who have insisted that God's law is eternal and must be kept by all men in all times, the label of legalist was branded upon them. My question is, what do you call the zealous Evangelicals who now are willing to go to prison in order to have the Ten Commandments placed in the public square? Perhaps they need to be reminded that it is not on tables of stone, but in their hearts that God's law must be written.

May God be praised for the awakening of these individuals. Their discovery has led them to come together under the banner of the Ten Commandments Commission. Ron Wexler, the chairman of this auspicious commission, makes the appeal, "… At a time when the Ten commandments are being banned from the public places, along with prayer, Scripture and expressions of faith, it is crucial for people of faith from all walks of life to take a bold stand for righteousness…that is what the Ten Commandments Commission is all about… to enable people to come together in unity and declare their commitment to God's holiness and righteousness…"

This amazing discovery of the Evangelical world demands a concerted decision with regard to the Sabbath commandment (Exodus 20:3-17). Their decision to uplift God's Ten Commandments as the moral foundation of the nation is a noble one. However, it creates a self-inflicted dilemma. God's holy law, which they are rightfully bringing to men's attention, explicitly states that His Sabbath is the seventh day of the week, today called Saturday. Nevertheless, almost the entire Christian world observes Sunday, the first day of the week, as the sabbath. Now that they have discovered the efficacy God's Ten Commandments, the question is, whose Sabbath will they honor? Will it be that of the God of creation, or will it be that of a man that claims to be God? This is a decision every Christian will personally have to make.

Ellen G. White, the world renown nineteenth century Christian commentator, writes rather prophetically, "...The Sabbath will be the great test of loyalty, for it is the point of truth especially controverted. When the final test shall be brought to bear upon men, then the line of distinction will be drawn between those who serve God and those who do not. While the observance of the false Sabbath in compliance with the law of the state, contrary to the fourth commandment, will be an avowal of allegiance to a power that is in opposition to God, the keeping of the true Sabbath, in obedience to God's law, is an evidence of loyalty to the Creator. While one class, by accepting the sign of submission to earthly powers, receive the mark of the beast, the other, choosing the token of allegiance to divine authority, receives the seal of God..." (**Great Controversy** pg. 605)

The newly elected pope, Benedict XVI, advances his church's determined effort for unity of all Christians. He exclaims, "... The commitment of the Catholic church to the search for Christian unity is irreversible..." (**USA Today**, June 27th 2005). That unity is rooted and grounded in Sunday sacredness. The love affair between Evangelicals and Catholics is truly a fulfillment of the Biblical prophecy of the whole world wondering after the beast. (Revelation 13:3)

But Scripture foretells that even in this climate of far-reaching apostasy, God will have a faithful remnant...there will yet be Protestants. John the Revelator prophesies, "...And the dragon was wroth with the woman and went to make war with the remnant of her seed, which keep the commandments of God and have the testimony of Jesus Christ..." (Revelation 12:17).

Which side of the battle are you on? Jesus assures us victory if we are on His side. The apostle John teaches, "...These have one mind, and shall give their power to the beast... These shall make war with the Lamb, and the Lamb shall overcome them: for He is Lord of Lords and

King of Kings: and they that are with Him are called, and chosen, and faithful…." (Revelation 17:13,14). By faith, you can and must choose the Lamb and be on His side.

Men have mended together various fig leaf garments of righteousness, with regards to the Sabbath. All of them are contrary what God's word teaches. In our next chapter, we will confront some of those popular objections and provide the correct Biblical answers.

CHAPTER 11

Confronting Objections to The Sabbath

Despite the incontrovertible evidence presented in this volume and the plain truth revealed in God's word, there are still those, who, while professing to be followers of Jesus Christ, flatly reject the truth about the Sabbath. Some even attempt to use the inspired word to support their false positions.

We will examine some of those arguments in this chapter. By the force of the Sacred word, the hollowness and folly of such arguments against God's Holy Sabbath-day will be exposed and rebuffed. It will be shown that those who advance such erroneous doctrines are themselves unskilled in and ignorant of the word of God.

The teaching of the heresy promoting the abolition of God's holy law, including the Sabbath commandment, is born out of ignorance or a selfish desire to satisfy one's earthly lusts. If men would but humble themselves before God and seek the guidance of the Holy Spirit, then they would see the Sabbath clearly and how God desires His people to relate to it.

Rejection of the clear teachings of the prophets and of Jesus, on the matter of the Sabbath, is the manifestation of a gross misunderstanding of Scripture. Particularly, they arise out of a convoluted presupposition of the apostle Paul's writings.

Plain Scriptures, particularly the writings of the apostle Paul, are twisted to establish erroneous positions. Other Scriptures are misquoted and misapplied in an attempt to justify the unscriptural doctrine of Sunday sacredness.

The apostle Peter, addressing this issue with regards to Paul's writings says, "…As also in all his (Paul's) epistles, speaking to them of these things; in which are some things hard to be understood, which they that are unlearned and unstable wrest as they do also the other Scriptures, unto their own destruction..." (2 Peter 3:16). Of such, Paul also writes, "...For when for the time ye ought to be teachers, ye have need that one teach you again which be the first principles of the oracles of God, and are become such as have need for milk and not of strong meat. For everyone that useth milk is unskillful in the word of righteousness for he is a babe...' (Hebrew 5:12-13).

Willingly or unwillingly, men's ignorance about the Sabbath is manifested in the many spurious theories they advocate. Let's look at the most popular of these and give the correct Biblical explanation thereof.

Creation week is not really seven literal days, but rather 7,000 years. Therefore, God could not be talking about a literal 7th day rest in the Sabbath Commandment.

What an insult to God and a disavowal of His inspired word. The passage of Scripture misused to justify this position reads thus, "...But, beloved, be not ignorant of this one thing, that one day is with the Lord as a thousand years, and a thousand years as one day..." (2 Peter 3:8).

Firstly, this Scripture is in no wise equating one day with one year. Peter's declaration is not a statement of comparison, but rather, one of contrast. He is simply contrasting our way of thinking with that of God's. He is echoing what the prophet Isaiah earlier stated, "...For my thoughts are nor your thoughts, neither are your ways my ways, saith the Lord, for as the heavens are higher than the earth, so are my thoughts higher than your thoughts..." (Isaiah 55:8,9).

Secondly, the subject of Peter's discourse is not creation. Instead, he is attempting to alleviate the doubts and fears of those who question another plainly revealed Bible truth, i.e. the visible, literal second coming to earth of our Lord and Savior, Jesus Christ. The apostle is assuring his hearers of the certainty of God's word in general, and the certainty of the second coming of Our Lord and Savior, Jesus Christ, in particular.

To justify their erroneous position, those who advance the thousand-year equals a day theory, also deny the literal, visible second coming of Jesus to the earth. That is what lies and error do. You always need one more lie to cover up the one before it.

A careful examination of Peter's discourse, which led him to make the statement of 2 Peter 3:8, would reveal that Peter, rather than equating a day with a thousand years at creation, is instead confirming the Biblical doctrine of the visible, literal second coming of Jesus.

Having given a detailed description of false teachers in the previous chapter (2 Peter 2), the apostle goes on to relate what will happen in the last days concerning the sure promise of the second coming of Jesus Christ. Peter teaches, "...Knowing this first, that there shall come in the last days scoffers, walking after their own lusts – and saying, where is the promise of His coming? For since the fathers fell asleep, all things continue as they were from the beginning of creation..." (2 Peter 3:3,4)

He continues to emphasize the certainty of the word of God. Peter points out the power of God's word in creation. He confirms the accuracy of prophecy in God foretelling and then destroying the antediluvians. He reiterates the resilience of God's word in holding the world together even to this day. Then Peter concludes that as sure as God's word was then, so it will be with respect to the coming of our Lord and Savior Jesus Christ.

If anything, this passage should serve to confirm the Sabbath rather than to deny it. For it demonstrates the assuredness and soundness of God's word from creation to this day.

The God of creation, who is also the God of the Sabbath, knew well that one day, men, ignorant of His word, willingly or not, would put forth this argument against His power of creation and the gift of His blessed Sabbath- day. So, at the end of each day of creation, God made the declaration, "...and the evening and the morning was the first day..." (Genesis 1:5). This is a 24 hour period, not unlike that which we have today.

How anyone can get 1000 years out of a morning and evening is beyond the faith and understanding of this writer. There are two questions that must be answered by those who promulgate this false theory. The first one is, how many years did they sleep last night? The second one is, where and when, in God's word, did He change the 24-hour day to 1000 years, and then change it back to 24 hours so that today we still have a 24-hour day? If those questions can be positively answered on he basis of God's word, then this theory can be established. If not, it must be flatly rejected. Additionally, how preposterous it is to believe that we must live for six thousand years and then rest for one thousand years. No human being has ever lived that long.

Plainly, this is a lie. God does not lie. This spurious doctrine is but a sophistry of the great deceiver, the father of lies. It is designed to turn away God's people from Him (God) and to deprive them of the blessings promised in His sanctified Sabbath-day.

Faith says that God created the heaven, the earth, the sea and everything in them in six literal days and rested on the seventh day. Human wisdom denies and replaces this plainly stated fact with its flawed and defective reasoning.

Nowhere in Scripture does God, the prophets or the apostles state that a day is the equivalent of 1000 years. This is a lie from the father of lies. Unfortunately, too many of God's people have been deceived into validating this heresy. Jesus Christ, our Creator, Savior, Redeemer and example did not in any way endorse such a teaching.

Finally, God does not need 1000 years to do anything. Time to Him is of no consequence. He affords us as much or as little as He deems necessary. The Psalmist David recognized this when he declared, "…For a thousand years in thy sight are but as yesterday when it is past and as a watch in the night…" (Psalm 90:4). This is the same thought that is expressed by the apostle Peter previously. It simply illustrates the contrast between God's thinking and ours.

With regards to creation, David declares, "…By the word of the Lord were the heavens made; and all the host of them by the breath of His mouth. He gathereth the waters of the sea together as an heap: He layeth up the depth in storehouses.… For He spake, and it was done, He commanded, and it stood fast…" (Psalm 33:6,7,9).

The prophet Isaiah is in complete agreement. He writes, "…I have declared the former things from the beginning; and they went forth out of My mouth, and I shewed them: I did them suddenly; and they came to pass…Mine hands also hath laid the foundations of the earth and My right hand hath spanned the heavens: when I called unto them, they stand up together…" (Isaiah 48:3,13).

One cannot avoid the Sabbath by claiming that God took six thousand years to create the world. Each week (seven days, not seven thousand years), the Sabbath comes around. One may deny it, but cannot avoid it. The Sabbath is an eternal oasis on the sands of time that appears every seven days. It calls all creation back to the one who created them, i.e. the God of the Sabbath.

Jesus rose from the dead on the first day of the week. So we honor it as the Lord's day and made it the Sabbath- day.

Here is a classical example of the devil's trickery of mixing truth with error, and passing it off as the Gospel to God's people. How sad that so many, claiming to be worshippers of the true God, are being led by the devil and his ministers of darkness into the pit of perdition.

The record is clear. Jesus was resurrected on the first day of the week, today called Sunday. All four of the Gospels record this account. Only one is needed to establish this fact, for they all agree perfectly. "…And when the Sabbath was past, Mary Magdalene and Mary the mother of James, and Salome, had brought sweet spices that they might come and anoint Him… And very early in the morning, the first day of the week, they came to the sepulchre at the rising of the sun… and he (the angel) said unto them, be not affrighted: ye seek Jesus of Nazareth, which was crucified: He is risen, He is not here: behold the place where they laid Him…" (Mark 16: 1,2,6).

This is truth. It is unadulterated truth. But this plain Bible truth is craftily twisted by the great deceiver. He now uses it, through his unwitting agents, to promote his false doctrine of Sunday sacredness.

It cannot be found, anywhere in Scripture, that because Jesus rose from the grave on the first day, that Sunday should be honored as a holy day, His day or the Sabbath-day. Neither Jesus, the prophets nor apostles taught such a doctrine. The origin of this heresy is in the twisted, perverted teachings of popery.

In the **Catechism of the Christian Doctrine and Practices**, we find this testimony:

Question: Why does the church command us to keep the Sunday holy instead of the Sabbath?

Answer: The church commands us to keep the Sunday holy instead of the Sabbath because on Sunday Christ rose from the dead, and on Sunday He sent the Holy Ghost upon the apostles.

The church may have commanded it; but God never sanctioned it. Jesus never commanded nor ordained that Sunday should be kept holy in honor of His resurrection. That doctrine, as was pointed out above, is a teaching of Roman Catholicism. She bequeaths it to her daughters, apostate Protestantism. They have nurtured, nourished ,reared and adores it like a well-beloved foster child.

Unfortunately, this spurious teaching is, though without Scriptural foundation, passionately embraced by almost all of Christianity. It has no basis in Scripture. As Protestants, we should regard the Holy Bible as our only guide of faith and practice. The apostle Paul sets the record straight. He plainly states, "...Therefore are we buried with Him by baptism into death: that like as Christ was raised up from the dead by the glory of the Father, even so we also should walk in the newness of life..." (Romans 6:4).

It is by the act of baptism that we commemorate Christ's resurrection. When we come out of the watery grave, we then honor Him by walking in the newness of life, as He walked. We can never do better than God. This is how He ordained it. It is what we should teach and practice.

Sunday sacredness in honor of Christ resurrection is a doctrine of the devil and a gross perversion of God's word. Any one, who professes Jesus Christ as their Lord and Savior, must reject it.

Some have gone so far as to denote Sunday as the Lord's Day. This error is just as dangerous, erroneous and deadly as the one that teaches that Sunday should be kept in honor of Christ's resurrection. Not surprisingly, they both came from the same source, the Church of Rome.

A twelfth century church historian, J.P. Migne, writes in his volume, **Patrologie**, "...All things whatsoever that was prescribed for the Bible Sabbath (the 7th day), we have transferred them to the Lord's day (the 1st day) as being authoritative and more highly regarded and the first in rank, and more honorable than the Jewish Sabbath..."

Sunday, to many, is perhaps a lord's day. It is certainly not the day of the Lord of creation. E.M. Chalmers writes in his book, '**How Sunday Came Into The Christian Church**', pg.3,"...The Gentile Christians of Rome and Alexandria began calling the first day of the week the lord's day. This was not difficult for the pagans of the Roman Empire who were steeped into sun worship to accept, because they (the pagans) referred to their sun-god as their lord..."

Our God makes it clear to His children what is His special day. God declares to Moses from Sinai, "...But the Seventh day is the Sabbath of the Lord thy God..." (Exodus 20:10). The prophet Isaiah likewise concludes, "...If you turn away thy foot from the Sabbath, from doing thy pleasure on My Holy day..." (Isaiah 58:13)

There is not a shadow of a doubt as to what God calls His Holy day. He calls it the Sabbath. It is the 7th day of the week, today called Saturday. God is the only one who can change it to Sunday, the first day of the week, and He never made such a change.

Moreover, our Lord and Savior, Jesus Christ, when accused by the Pharisees of breaking the Sabbath, declared, "...The Sabbath was made for man, and not man for the Sabbath, therefore the Son of Man is Lord also of the Sabbath..." (Mark 2:27, 28)

It cannot be established, from God's word, that the Lord's day is any other day but the Sabbath-day, the seventh day of the week.

To attempt to assign the sanctity of the seventh day to any other day is to act in bold defiance of the God of Creation. Such an act is asserting that one is greater than God. It is usurping God's position as ruler of the universe. It is anti-Christian. God blessed, hallowed and sanctified His holy day, the Sabbath of creation. No one can change that.

Finally, to change one's will after they are dead is illegal. Sunday keeping, as was already pointed out, was established in the Christian church some three hundred years after the death of Jesus Christ.

To presume to change His will of keeping the seventh-day Sabbath, claiming the first day to be holy because He rose on that day, is a violation of His will. Any attempt at such a change is therefore illegal and of no effect.

God's law, including the Sabbath Commandment, was nailed to the cross. Therefore, we no longer have to keep the law.

What a frightening thought?

As was pointed out in an earlier chapter, it is impossible for God to negate His law in anyway. It is the most satanic of doctrines to teach that He did so by nailing it to the cross at Jesus' crucifixion. Such a teaching defies basic common sense and cannot be established by the word of God. God's word gives no such revelation.

God's law is the very foundation of His government. It is His constitution, laid down for all men, in all times to obey. His law is the expression of His will. God's law provides the norms and defines the parameters by which He expects us, His children, to live. It is the most ridiculous notion to suggest that it was done away with at the cross. Why would Jesus pay such a price, die such an ignominious death in order to rid the world of the law of God? The plain answer is that He did no such thing. To do so would be an act of insanity and Jesus was not insane.

Quite to the contrary, Jesus declared,"...Think not that I am come to destroy the law or the prophets. I am not come to destroy but to fulfill. For verily I say unto you till heaven and earth pass, one jot or tittle shall in no wise pass from the law, till all be fulfilled. Whosoever therefore shall break one of these least commandments, and shall teach men so, he shall be called the least in the kingdom of heaven: but whosoever shall do and teach them, the same shall be called great in the kingdom of heaven..." (Matthew 5:17-19). Jesus' job is to empower us to keep the law. He has not given anyone authorization to break or destroy His law, and He most certainly did not do away with it.

The Scripture text that men erroneously use to justify this unscriptural position is this, "...Blotting out the handwriting of ordinances that was against us, and took it out of the way, nailing it to the cross... Let no man therefore judge you in meat, or drink, or in respect of an holy day, or of the new moon, or of the Sabbath days....

which are a shadow of things to come; but the body of Christ..."
(Colossians 2:14, 16, 17)

Upon careful examination of these texts, we discover the following: (1) The texts refer to the handwriting of ordinances which were against us. (2) Paul admonishes the newly baptized Jews not to judge anyone according to the meat and drink offerings, and the feast days associated with the ancient sanctuary services and ceremonies. (3) Paul says that those ordinances, including circumcision and the yearly feast days, which were called Sabbaths, were to be fulfilled in the life and ministry of Jesus Christ.

There is no mention here of the Ten Commandment law. All men in all times are subject to that law. Paul declares, "...Wherefore the law is holy, and the commandment holy, and just, and good..."(Romans 7:12). Certainly, Paul was making no reference to the 7th day Sabbath, the very seal of God's law, when he talked about the ordinances in Colossians 2:11-17. He reiterates, "...Circumcision is nothing, uncircumcision is nothing, but the keeping of the Commandments of God..." (1Corinthians 7:19).

Paul continues, dealing with the same issue, in the book of Hebrews, "...Then verily, the first covenant had also ordinances of divine service, and a worldly sanctuary (Hebrews 9:1). The learned apostle goes on, "...Which stood only in meats and drinks, and divers washings, and carnal ordinances, imposed on them until the time of reformation...but Christ being come an High Priest of good things to come, by a greater and more perfect tabernacle, not made with hands, that is to say, not of this building..." (Hebrews 9:10-11)

When we examine the Sacred word, we discover that there were two sets of laws which God used Moses to share with the people of Israel, relative to their worship experience.

First, there was the Ten Commandment law. (Exodus 20:1-17). It was written on tables of stone with God's own hand. The record reveals, "...And He (God) gave unto Moses, when He had made an end of communing with him upon Mount Sinai, two tables of stone, written with the finger of God..." (Exodus 31:18). Further, God instructed Moses where to place the Ten Commandment law. God directed Moses,

"...And thou shall put into the ark of the testimony which I shall give thee..." (Exodus 25:16). Moses, being an obedient servant, did exactly what God asked him to do.

God again commanded Moses, "...And I will write on the tables the words that were in the first tables which thou breakest, and thou shalt put them in the ark..." (Deuteronomy 10:2).
Again, Moses humbly obeyed. "...And I turned myself and came down from the mount, and put the tables in the ark which I had made and there they be, as the Lord commanded me..." (Deuteronomy 10:5).

Clearly, it was the Ten Commandment law (Exodus 20:1- 17), written by the finger of God, and placed by Moses in the ark, that is here referred to.

Secondly, there was the handwriting of ordinances relating to the sanctuary and its services. That was a shadow of Jesus Christ's life and ministry.

Moses tells us also about that law. "...And It came to pass, when Moses had made an end of writing the words of this law in a book, until they were finished, that Moses commanded the Levites which bare the ark of the covenant of the Lord saying... take this book of the law, and put it in the side of the ark of the covenant of the Lord your God, that it may be there for a witness against thee..." (Deuteronomy 31:24-26).

Here we find a law, separate and distinct from the Ten Commandments, being referred to. This law was written by the hand of Moses and not by the finger of God. It was not written on tables of stone, but in a book. It was placed on the side of the ark and not inside the ark. Those laws outlined the instructions for the people of ancient Israel to follow in relation to the sanctuary and its services. They had to do with rites, rituals and ceremonies connected with the sanctuary services.

So we read, for example, "...And the meat offerings thereof shall be two tenth deal of fine flour mingled with oil, an offering made by fire unto the Lord for a sweet savor; and the drink offering thereof shall be of wine, the fourth part of an hin..." (Leviticus 23:13).

The book of Leviticus gives a thorough account of those ordinances and ceremonies..

In his message to the converts at Colossae, Paul was admonishing the saints, both Jews and Gentiles, that these feasts, sacrifices and ceremonies were no longer necessary. Paul rightly taught that they were figures and shadows of events to be fulfilled in the life and ministry of Jesus Christ. And indeed they were.

Further, in the book of Hebrews, Paul gives the most thorough explanation of the doctrine of the ancient sanctuary and its services as it relates to the ministry, sacrifice and High Priestly office of Jesus Christ. This is a subject that every Christian needs to understand fully.

God's Plan of redemption is best understood in the context of the sanctuary. Hence, the psalmist Asaph admonishes us, "…Thy way, O God, is in the sanctuary: who is so great a god as our God…" (Psalm 77:13).David likewise declares,"… They have seen thy goings of my God, my King, in the sanctuary…" (Psalm 68:24).

The ancient sanctuary and its services were an object lesson on the plan of salvation for men's souls. God gave it to the Israelites as a means of teaching them who He was and what His plan for their salvation was all about. So, God tells Moses, "… Let them make me a sanctuary; that I may dwell among them…" (Exodus 25:8).

Here are explanations of the feasts days and their fulfillment in the life and ministry of Jesus Christ.

Passover/Unleavened Bread.
"…The fourteenth day of the first month at even is the Lord's Passover … and on the fifteenth day of the same month is the feast of unleavened bread unto the Lord…" (Leviticus 23:5-6)
Fulfillment in Jesus Christ.
"…Purge out therefore the old leaven, that ye may be a new lump as ye are unleavened. For even Christ our Passover is sacrificed for us…" (I Corinthians 5:7)

First fruits.
"…Speak unto the children of Israel, and say unto them, when ye come into the land which I give unto you, ye shall reap the harvest thereof, then ye shall bring a sheaf of the first fruits of your harvest unto the

priest... and ye shall wave the sheaf before the Lord to be accepted for you..." (Leviticus 23:10-11)
Fulfillment in Jesus Christ.
"...But now is Christ risen from the dead, and become the first fruit of them that slept... But every man in his own order: Christ the first fruits; afterward they that are Christ at his coming..." (1Corinthains 15:20,23)

Pentecost.
"...And ye shall count unto you from the morrow after the Sabbath from the day that ye brought the sheaf of the wave offering; seven Sabbaths shall be complete: Even unto the morrow after the seventh Sabbath shall ye number fifty days; and ye shall offer a new meat offering unto the Lord..." (Leviticus 23:15, 16) NOTE: The gift of the Holy Ghost was given to the disciples by Christ fifty days after his resurrection.
Fulfillment in Jesus Christ
"... And when the day of Pentecost were fully come, they were all with one accord in one place... and suddenly there came a sound from heaven as a mighty rushing wind, and it filled the house where they were sitting... and they were filled with the Holy Ghost, and began to speak with other tongues, as the Spirit gave them utterance..." (Acts 1:1, 2, 4).

Trumpets/Atonement.
"...Speak unto the children of Israel, saying, in the seventh month, in the feast day of the month, shall ye have a Sabbath, a memorial of blowing trumpets in holy convocation... Also on the tenth day of this seventh month, there shall be a day of atonement. It shall be a holy convocation unto you; and ye shall afflict your souls and offer an offering made by fire unto the Lord..." (Leviticus 23:24, 27). NOTE: The call to come back to the worship of the true God, the God of creation, the God of the Sabbath, goes out to all humanity today.
Fulfillment in Jesus Christ.
"...And I saw another angel fly in the midst of heaven, having the everlasting gospel to preach unto them that dwell upon the earth, and to every nation, and kindred, and tongue and people... saying with a loud

voice, 'fear God and give glory to Him; for the hour of His judgment is come: and worship Him that made the heaven and earth, and the sea, and the fountain of waters...'." (Revelation 14: 6,7)

Tabernacles/Ingathering.
"...Speak unto the children of Israel, saying, the fifteenth day of this seventh month shall be the feast of tabernacles (ingathering) for seven days unto the Lord... Also in the fifteenth day of the seventh month, when ye have gathered in the fruit of the land, ye shall keep a feast unto the Lord seven days: on the first day shall be a Sabbath and on the eight day shall be a Sabbath... Ye shall dwell in the booths seven days, all that are Israelites born shall dwell in booths..." (Leviticus 23:39, 42) NOTE: The Feast of the Tabernacles/Booths foreshadowed the return of Jesus Christ to earth to gather His elect and to take them to heaven for 1000 years. As the Jews returned to their homes after the feast, so will the people of God return to an earth made new, after the thousand years, to spend the ceaseless ages of eternity with Him. (Revelation 20:4)(Matthew 5:5)

Fulfillment in Jesus Christ
"...For the Lord Himself shall descend from heaven with a shout, with the voice of the archangel, and with the trump of God; and the dead in Christ shall rise first, then we which are alive and remain shall be caught up together with them in the clouds, to meet the Lord in the air: and so shall we ever be with the Lord... And I saw thrones, and they that sat upon them, and Judgment was given unto them. And I saw the souls of them which were beheaded for the witness of Jesus, and for the word of God, and which had not worshipped the beast, neither his image, neither had received the mark upon their foreheads, or in their hands; and they lived and reigned with Christ a thousand years..." (1 Thessalonians 4:16, 17) (Revelation 20:4, Revelation 21:1-4).

It was to these feasts that the apostle Paul was referring in his letter to the Colossians, Chapter 2 verses 11-17. They were indeed shadows of the life and ministry of Christ. They were God's object lesson In the plan of salvation for the people of Israel. Through that system, the people were to get a clear picture of God's plan of redemption for their lives. They taught the seriousness of sin and showed God's mercy for sinners.

Those feast days, with the exception of the feast of Tabernacles, have been or are in the process of being fulfilled. We are living in the antitypical Day of Atonement. It is a time of cleansing and of judgment. This is why, as Christians, we must return to the keeping of all of God's commandments, including the Sabbath commandment. This is the time to make it right with God by keeping all of His commandments. It should be a time of great soul searching.

All cases are judged and decided on the basis of God's Ten Commandments. They are His standard of righteousness and judgment (James 2:12).

Paul confirms, "...Which was a figure for the time then present, in which were offered both gifts and sacrifices, that could not make him that did the service perfect, as pertaining to the conscience... which stood only in meats and drinks, and divers washings, and carnal ordinances, imposed on them until the time of reformation... But Christ being an High Priest of good things to come, by a greater and more perfect tabernacle, not made with hands, that is to say not of this building... Neither by the blood of goats and calves, but his own blood he entered in once into the holy place, having obtainedeternal salvation for us..." (Hebrews 9:9-12).

The feasts discussed by Paul were indeed a shadow of things to come. Those feasts days, called Sabbath-days, could have been any day of the week. In no way was Paul in his discourse referring to "the Sabbath-day", the 7th day of the week.

Jesus at His crucifixion confirmed what Paul was teaching in Colossians 2 and Hebrews 9. Those types and symbols were indeed nailed to the cross. Matthew reports, "...And behold the veil of the temple was rent in twain from the top to the bottom: and the earth did quake, and the rocks rent, and graves were opened; and many bodies of the saints which slept arose..." (Matthew 27:51, 52). This signified the end of the ceremonial and sacrificial system to which Paul referred. They were thus nailed to the cross. Finally, Paul teaches, "...What shall we say then? Is the law sin? God forbid. Nay. I had not known sin, but by the law; for I had not known lust, except the law had said, 'Thou shalt not covet..."(Romans 7:7).

The law which tells us not to covet is the same law that admonishes us to keep the Sabbath-day holy. If that law is done away with, then how would we know what sin is? We have no other standard by which to truly determine what sin is. Since there is still sin in the world, then the law must also still exist. Sin is the transgression of the law. (1John 3:4).

As we answer the next objection, you will discover that indeed the seventh-day Sabbath was not nailed to the cross. It was, most definitely, observed by the disciples and the early church long after Christ's death and resurrection.

The disciples ceased to keep the Sabbath-day and kept Sunday as the Lord's Day.

We have pointed out in a previous chapter, who it was that attempted to change God's law. It was not the disciples and certainly it was not Jesus. It was, as was clearly demonstrated, the Roman Papacy. No one can change God's law. They may attempt to do so, but they will never succeed.

Paul declared,"...The God and the Father of our Lord Jesus, which is blessed for evermore, knoweth that I lie not..." (2 Corinthians 11:31). The apostate prophet Balaam also recognized this fact. He exclaimed, "...Behold, I have received commandment to bless: and He (God) hath blessed; and I cannot reverse it..." (Numbers 23:20). The writer of the Chronicles likewise agreed, "...Now therefore let it please thee to bless the house of thy servant, that it may be before thee forever. For thou blessest, O Lord, and it shall be blessed forever..." (1 Chronicles 17:27).

The seventh-day Sabbath was blessed and sanctified by God at creation. It is therefore blessed and holy forever. No man can curse or change it.

Jesus Christ, at no time during His three and one half years of prophetic ministry on earth, gave any instruction that after his death the Sabbath will be changed to Sunday. We have already dealt with thetheory that because Christ rose on Sunday, the first day of the week, that day became the Sabbath or the Lord's day. Further, we pointed the reader to the one with whom that false doctrine originated and by whom it is being promulgated.

To the contrary, Jesus told His disciples that the Sabbath would be kept even after His death. In foretelling the destruction of Jerusalem and the end of the world, the Messiah exclaimed, "…But pray ye that your flight be not in the winter neither on the Sabbath-day…" (Matthew24:20). How careful was the Savior to warn His followers, that even the destruction of their city or the crisis at the end of the world, should not interfere with the sanctity of the Sabbath and their obligation to keep it holy.

Immediately after Jesus' crucifixion, the disciples were adamant in keeping the Sabbath. They would not as much as anoint the body of their Savior for burial on the holy Sabbath-day. Luke records, "…And that day was the preparation day, and the Sabbath drew on… And they returned, and prepared spices and ointments and rested on the Sabbath day according to the commandment…" (Luke 23: 54, 56).

The record firmly states that rather than changing or abandoning the Sabbath, on account of Jesus' death and burial, the disciples continued to honor it as the Lord's day.

What of this notion that the disciples gathered together on the first day of the week to celebrate the Lord's resurrection? The apostle John disputes that allegation. He writes, "…Then the same day at evening, being the first day of the week, when the doors were shut, where the disciples were assembled for fear of the Jews, came Jesus and stood in the midst, and said unto them, Peace be unto you…" (John 20:19)

This was no Sunday convocation in honor of Jesus' resurrection. In fact, the disciples present were not aware of Jesus' resurrection until He appeared unto them. The Scripture makes it abundantly clear that they were gathered, not to hold a church service, but because they were afraid of the Jews. The disciples feared that the same treatment would be meted out to them as was meted out to their Master, Jesus Christ.

Citing the passage in Acts 20:17 which reads,"…And upon the

first day of the week, when the disciples came together to break bread, Paul preached unto them, ready to depart on the morrow; and continued his speech until midnight...", some claim this to be proof that the disciples changed the Sabbath to Sunday. They assert that this meeting signaled the ushering in of the New Covenant.

The New Covenant simply states that God would write His laws (the Ten Commandments) on the hearts of His people. It did not state that God would do away with His law or change it in anyway. (Hebrews 8:7-10). The New Covenant was ushered in by the sacrifice of Jesus and not by a meeting of His disciples on the first day of the week.

First of all, there is no indication, implication or assertion that a change from the seventh day to the first was made.

Secondly, we are told that it was the custom of the disciples to come together everyday of the week to break bread, i.e. to fellowship. Physician Luke writes, "...And they (the disciples) continuing daily with one accord in the temple, and breaking bread from house to house, did eat their meat with gladness and singleness of heart..." (Acts 2:46).

Thirdly, the Bible teaches us that the day begins at evening, "... And the evening and the morning were the first day..." (Genesis 1:5). It is therefore clear, from the passage in Acts 20:7, that this meeting was the continuation of a Sabbath gathering that prolonged into the evening (beginning of the first day). It was not a Sunday service celebrating the resurrection of our Lord. It was, most assuredly, not an indication of any change of the Sabbath from the seventh day to the first. Besides, the Covenants, old and new, are God's Covenants and not the disciples'. It is therefore impossible and illegal for them or anyone else to change them. Only the God of creation can do that. Thanks be to Him for never changing it.

Another passage, used by the opponents of God's Sabbath, to justify Sunday sacredness, is the one found in the book of I Corinthians 16:1, 2 which reads, "...Now concerning the collection for the saints, as I have order to the churches of Galatia, even so do ye... upon the first day of the week let everyone of you lay by him in store, as God hath prospered him, that there be no gatherings when I come..."

Here, Paul is specifically instructing the saints that there will be no gathering on the first day. He was simply informing the brethren to lay aside their offerings to be given to the church at Jerusalem. Paul wanted the offerings to available on Sunday after the Sabbath was passed. There is no change here from Sabbath to Sunday. Further, we find that not only did the apostles not change God's holy day from the seventh day to the first; but indeed they continued to honor it in every particular.

Luke again records, "...And when they (Paul and Barnabas) departed from Perga, they came to Antioch in Pisidia and went into the synagogue on the Sabbath-day and sat down..." (Acts 13:14). He continues, "...And when the Jews were gone out of the synagogue, the Gentiles besought that these words might be preached to them the next Sabbath..." (Acts 13:42).

The question now arises: If the Sabbath was changed to Sunday by the disciples, why did the Gentiles not request that Paul meet with them the next day, Sunday? The plain answer is that neither the Jews nor the Gentiles were sanctioning any change from the seventh day to the first day. Paul honored their request. Luke relates, "...And the next Sabbath day came almost the whole city together to hear the word of God..."(Acts 13:44).

Paul, having no knowledge of the Sabbath being changed to Sunday, continued his ministry in the manner which God had ordained, honoring God's Sabbath. Luke again records,
"...And on the Sabbath, we went out of the city by the riverside, where prayer was wont to be made; and we sat down and spake unto the women which resorted thither..." (Acts 16:13).

Paul, a minister of the Gospel of grace and an ardent proponent of keeping all of God's Holy law, did not abandon the Sabbath commandment. He kept it the way he knew God had ordained it. He was a commandment keeping Jew who continued to keep and teach God's law when He became a Christian. He made the clear distinction, which most Christians seem to avoid or are ignorant of, that there were two sets of laws with regards to the worship experience of God's people. One, the ceremonial laws, which were indeed nailed to the cross; and the other, the moral law (the Ten Commandments), which are eternally binding upon all men for all times.

Again Luke records, "...And Paul, as his manner was, went in unto them on the Sabbath day and reasoned with them out of the Scriptures..." (Acts 17:2). Paul continued in obedience to the Lord's command,"...And he reasoned in the synagogue every Sabbath, and persuaded the Jews and the Gentiles..." (Acts 18:4).

This claim from Sabbath to Sunday is un-Biblical and groundless. We have shown, in an earlier chapter, whose work it was and is to force that change upon God's people.

Paul teaches that we may choose whatever day we want, so long as we choose one day in seven to rest.

How absurd.

To comfort and confirm themselves in this erroneous doctrine, its proponents cite Paul's writings in the book of Romans. "...One man esteemeth one day above another: another esteemeth every day alike. Let everyman be fully persuaded in his own mind. He that regardeth the day regardeth it unto the Lord; and he that regardeth not the day to the Lord he doth not regard it. He that eateth, eateth to the Lord, for he giveth God thanks, and he that eateth not to the Lord, he eateth not, and giveth God thanks..." (Romans 14:5-6). Nowhere in this passage, or any other place in this chapter does Paul refer to the keeping of the Sabbath-day.

It has already been proved that Paul, along with the other disciples, kept holy God's seventh-day Sabbath after the death and resurrection of Jesus Christ. To now subscribe to the notion, that Paul is here teaching the church to observe whatever day they choose, in honor of God's Sabbath, is self-contradictory heresy of the highest order. Paul is not a teacher of heresy. Neither does he contradict the teachings of Jesus or the prophets. Our God, the Creator, the God of the Sabbath is not a God of confusion. He is a God of order and specificity. To suggest that each one may keep the Sabbath on whatever day he chooses is confusion. This is exactly what we have in the religious world. God calls this confusion Babylon.

A close examination of this passage of Scripture (Romans 14:1-

23) reveals that Paul, contrary to talking about a Holy day as some men teach, is discussing food and fasting. Paul is admonishing the saints that they should not judge another based upon the foods that he eats or the days on which he chooses fasts. Notice also, that Paul never said that we can and should eat anything we choose.

Every Christian is at a different point on his/her Christian experience. Paul is essentially saying that we should not judge another based upon what we have overcome. Rather, we should help each other overcome and attain, as God would have us attain in the matter of diet. Our relationship with our fellow man must not be based upon what they eat or do not eat; but rather upon love and righteousness.

God has already shown us in His word what is permissible for human consumption and what is not (See Leviticus chapter 11). Some may have attained, and some may not. God has not given the job of judging those who have not attained to those who have. This was the central theme of Paul's discourse in this passage.

The other point, upon which Paul touched, is the matter of fast days. It was, and still is a Jewish custom, that each one chooses two days of fasting per week. Men were free to choose which day(s) they fasted on. This is what Paul is addressing in verse 5. Further, Paul admonishes that whatever day one chooses, he must be fully convinced in his mind that that is what God wants of him. For the act of fasting is not unto men, but unto God.

This principle is brought out clearly in the parable of the Pharisee and the publican. Jesus gives the illustration of two men, one a Pharisee and the other a publican, going into the temple to pray. The Pharisee proceeded to tell God how good he was and the many good deeds he does. One of those good deeds, Jesus relates, is fasting. The record reads, "…I fast twice in the week, I give tithes of all that I possess…" (Luke 18:12). The publican, recognizing his need for the Savior, simply said, "…God be merciful to me a sinner…" (Luke 18:13). This is indeed what we all need to do.

Paul, in Romans Chapter 14, does not in any way address the issue of Sabbath keeping. He most certainly did not give license for anyone to change God's holy Sabbath-day. The apostle Paul was a most astute student of the Word. He knew well this saying, "...For I am the Lord, I change not..." (Malachi 3:6).

Truly God has not changed His position on the sanctity of the Sabbath and man's requirement to keep it holy. Scripture does not teach such a doctrine. It is a device of the devil advanced by his agents, masquerading as servants of God. It is a deception. God's people must reject it.

The foregoing arguments by no means answer every objection to the Sabbath. They, however, along with the other information and documentation presented in this volume, prove the everlasting nature and eternal blessings of holding the seventh-day Sabbath in its proper perspective as we journey along the Christian pathway. The proper perspective is for Christians to keep it holy as God has commanded.

In our next chapter we will show you how, by God's grace, you can choose Jesus and His blessed Sabbath-day. In doing so, you will reject the darkness of Sunday sacredness, which is the mark of the beast.

CHAPTER 12
The Sabbath And Righteousness By Faith

The apostle Paul tells us very clearly that, "...For therein is the righteousness of God revealed from faith to faith: as it is written the just shall live by faith..." (Romans 1:17). To properly comprehend the true meaning of this passage of Scripture, one must have a clear understanding of what is righteousness and what is faith.

Man's own subjective explanation will not help us in determining the true meaning of righteousness or faith. So, we turn to the only reliable explanation available to us all, i.e. the word of God. The Psalmist David explains, "...My tongue shall speak of thy word: for all thy commandments are righteousness..." (Psalm 119:172). The apostle Paul records, "...Abraham believed God, and it was counted unto him for righteousness..." (Romans 4:3). Abraham's belief in God was not just a mental assent to what God had said. Abraham's belief in God was manifested in his acting upon what God had commanded.

The Scripture records that Abraham not only left the comfort of his own country and kinsfolk to go to an unknown place where God had commanded him to go; but he also was willing to sacrifice his own son as God had ordered (Genesis ch.12 & ch.22).

Righteousness, therefore, is the obeying of God's commands. It is submitting to God's will, regardless of how we feel or what other men may say. God's will is found in His word. It cannot be obtained from the traditions of men. Our belief in God is manifested by our willingness to obey His word. That is faith.

We can only obey God if we have faith in Him. Paul again

declares, "...But without faith it is impossible to please Him (God): for he that cometh to God must believe that He is, and the He is the rewarder of them that diligently seek Him..." (Hebrews 11:6).

Paul does not leave it to us to speculate on what is this thing called faith. He tells us quite plainly,"...Now faith is the substance of things hoped for, the evidence of things not seen..." (Hebrews 11:1).

Faith, therefore, is the foundation of our entire Christian experience. Beginning from the first words of Holy Writ, "...In the beginning, God created the heaven and the earth..." (Genesis 1:1) to the very last pronouncement: "...The grace of our Lord Jesus Christ be with you all, Amen..." (Revelation 22:21), faith is demanded of us. It is the only foundation upon which our Christian experience can be built.

We were not present when God created the world, neither are we yet present when He will make all things new. It is only by faith that we accept these things. It is by that faith that we live, moment by moment, day by day.

If our faith enables us to believe that God created the heaven and the earth and all that is in them; and if our faith prompts us to believe that God will make all things new, then our life today must also be rooted and grounded in that faith. True faith is simply trusting God on the basis of what He has revealed in His word.

That faith is centered in our only Savior from sin, Jesus Christ, Our Lord. He tells us, "...I am the way, the truth, and the life: no man cometh unto the Father, but by me..." (John 14:6).

Jesus' attitude towards God's law was that He kept them perfectly. His own words testify to that undeniable fact. He declares, "...If ye keep my commandments, ye shall abide in my love; even as I have kept my Father's commandments and abide in His love..." (John 15:10).

The commandments to which He refers are the Ten Commandments. They are the moral standard for all men in all times. Jesus' faith in His Father was demonstrated in His keeping all of His Father's commandments.

Those commandments include the Sabbath Commandment. Thus the apostle Luke reports, "...And He (Jesus) came to Nazareth where He had been brought up; and, as His custom was, He went into

the synagogue on the Sabbath day and stood up for to read..." (Luke 4:16). Luke continues,
"...And He (Jesus) came down to Capernaum, a city of Galilee, and taught them on the Sabbath-day..." (Luke 4:31). In a previous chapter, we showed that Jesus followed His Father's command to keep the Sabbath holy. He has left us the only example we should follow in this regard. By faith, we should follow Him even as He followed His Father.

As Jesus' faith in His Father's words left Him no choice but to obey, so must our faith be in Jesus. We must follow Him where He leads us. Jesus pleads with us, "...Come unto me, all ye that labor and are heavy laden and I will give you rest... take My yoke upon you and learn of me: for I am meek and lowly in heart: and ye shall find rest unto your souls...For My yoke is easy, and my burden is light..." (Matthew 11:28–30).

The yoke here mentioned is likened unto an agricultural implement. In agrarian societies, such as existed in Jesus' time, a yoke was placed around the necks of two animals, one younger, the other, more mature. The idea was that wherever the more mature animal, usually an ox, went, so would the younger animal. The younger animal had no other choice. Jesus uses this metaphor to illustrate the relationship He desires us to have with Him. He is beckoning us to become yoked up with Him. When we do, we will go wherever He goes, whenever He goes.

It has already been pointed out that Jesus kept His Father's law perfectly. As you become yoked up with Jesus by faith, your life will reflect His life. With respect to the Sabbath, we must therefore follow Him in keeping it holy. We must imitate Him in keeping all of God's commandments. If we but yield our hearts to Him, He will empower us to abide in His will. If we truly love Him, then we would have no problem obeying Him. The Savior admonishes us, "...If ye love me, keep my commandments..." (John 14:15).If your faith truly is in Jesus, then the Sabbath command would be a delight for you to obey. With faith in Jesus, keeping His Sabbath command is not a burden. It is always a pleasure and blessing to obey God, in the person of His Son Jesus Christ. The apostle John reminds us, "...By this we know that we love the children of God, when we love God and keep His commandments. For this is the love of God, that we keep His commandments, and His commandments are not grievous..." (1John 5:2,3).

True love and faith in Jesus is manifested by the life that one lives. It should be a life lived in accordance with His commandments. Those commandments include His Sabbath command, which says, "...Remember the Sabbath Day to keep it holy. Six days shall thou labor and do all thy work: by the seventh day (not the first) is the Sabbath of the Lord thy God: in it thou shalt not do any work: thou, nor thy son, nor thy daughter ,nor thy man servant nor thy maid servant, nor thy cattle, nor thy stranger that is within thy gates: for in six days, the Lord made heaven and the earth, the sea and all that in them is, and rested the seventh day: wherefore the Lord blessed the Sabbath-day, and hallowed it..." (Exodus 20:8-11).

What child of God would want to reject such a blessing? It is a blessing that can come only from the Creator. If you have faith enough to believe that God is your Creator, then your faith ought also to motivate you to accept and keep holy His Sabbath-day.

Keeping the Sabbath-day holy is not a laundry list of do's and don'ts. It is not a senseless round of rites and rituals. Rather, the Sabbath is a constant reminder of who your Creator is.

With unwavering consistency, the Sabbath comes around every seven days. It is the eternal reminder of God's manifold blessings toward us during the previous six days. Through His gift of the Sabbath-day, God wants us to remember who He is. He gently asks us to rest from our labor. He has given us the example at Creation. We remember and keep the Sabbath as evidence of the fact that we do truly believe that God is our Creator.

For the Christian, the Sabbath should be a time of joyous passion. It should be a time of divine reflection welcomed with hallowed anticipation. Resting from our labors on the seventh day, as God has commanded, is the out working of our faith in God as our Creator. It is a time in which we pause to reflect upon His blessings in the last six days, and be recharged for the journey of the next six days.

Like baptism, which is an outworking of our faith in Jesus as our Redeemer, the Sabbath is the outworking of our faith in God, as our Creator. It is the clearest evidence that we indeed worship the true God, the God of Creation.

The apostle James illustrates the issue of faith. He declares, "…Even so faith, if it had not works, is dead, being alone… yea, a man may say, thou hast faith, and I have works: shew me thy faith without thy works, and I will shew thee my faith by my works…Thou believest that there is one God (the Creator) thou doest well: the devils also believe and tremble… But wilt thou know, O vain man, that faith without works is dead…" (James 2:17-20).

Such is the man that says he loves Jesus and claims God as His Creator, yet blatantly rejects that precious gift of God's holy Sabbath-day.

Of such a one, the apostle John writes, "…He that saith I know Him, and keepeth not His commandments, is a liar and the truth is not in him…" (1 John 2:4). Of liars, Jesus declares, "…Ye are of your father the devil, and the lust of your father ye will do. He was a murderer from the beginning, and abode not in the truth, because there is no truth in him. When he speaketh a lie, he speaketh of his own: for he is a liar and the father of it…" (John 8:44).

Sunday sacredness is a lie from the father of lies. God's seventh-day Sabbath is the truth as it is in Jesus. It is truth, like all other Bible truths, whether we agree with it or not. We must accept it by faith. Jesus tells the woman at the well, "…But the hour cometh, and now is when the true worshipper shall worship the Father in spirit and in truth: for the Father seeketh such to worship Him… God is spirit: and they that worship Him must worship Him in Spirit and in truth…"(John 4:23-24). King David explains what is that truth,"…Thy righteousness is an everlasting righteousness, and thy law is truth…" (Psalm 119:142).

Too often, the experience of Christians is steeped in ecstatic emotional manifestations, abstract concepts of God and total ignorance of what God requires of their lives. What God requires is righteousness. Righteousness is the keeping of God's law. It comes only by possessing an abiding, unyielding faith in His word. "…All unrighteousness is sin…and there is a sin not unto death…"(1 John 5:17).

The only sin, which is not unto death, is the sin of ignorance.

James declares, "...Therefore, to him that knoweth to do good, and doeth it not, it is sin..." (James 4:17). Luke shines further light on the matter. "... At the times of ignorance God winked at; but now commands all men everywhere to repent..." (Acts 17:30).

If you have read this book to this point, you cannot claim ignorance for not trusting God and obeying His command to keep the Sabbath-day holy. If you own a Bible, you cannot claim ignorance of God's requirement for His blessed Sabbath-day. The truth of this matter is plainly put forth, not only in this volume but also in your Bible. In fact, this volume is based solely on the Bible, God's holy word.

Unrighteousness is sin, and sin is the breaking of God's law. "...Whosoever committeth sin transgresseth also the law: for sin is the transgression of the law..." (1 John 3:4). The penalty for sin is death. Paul writes, "...For the wages of sin is death..." (Romans 6:23). But thanks to God, Paul did not stop there. He pointed us to the solution. He continues, "...but the gift of God is eternal life through Jesus Christ our Lord ..." (Romans 6:23).

This gift of eternal life is attainable. However, it cannot be attained merely by proclaiming lip service acceptance of Jesus. It can only be achieved by having an abiding, living faith in Jesus Christ. Such faith leads to righteousness. It is a faith that motivates us to keep all of His commandments, including His Sabbath command.

Paul speaks of this faith that leads to righteousness, "...I am crucified with Christ, nevertheless I live, yet not I but Christ liveth in me; and the life which I now live in the flesh, I live by the faith of the Son of God, who loved me and give Himself for me..." (Galatians 2:20)

And what was that life that Christ lived? Paul answers, "...For we have not an High Priest which cannot be touched with the feeling of our infirmities; but was in all points tempted like as we are, yet without sin..." (Hebrews 4:15).

Jesus, Paul declares, kept the law perfectly. Peter says that Jesus is our example, "...For even hereunto were ye called: because Christ also suffered for us, leaving us an example, that ye should follow his steps..." (1 Peter 2:21)

His life, His example and His steps testify, without any shadow of a doubt, that He kept His Father's law completely. By faith in Him we can do likewise.

As our Savior, Jesus kept the law flawlessly during His sojourn among us upon earth. He did not live and give up His life on Calvary's hill so that we might abandon His law and live unrighteously. The grace by which He saves us is also the power which he imparts to us. He imparts it to us so that we may keep His law. We keep it not in our own strength, but in His only. Paul assures us, "…I can do all things through Christ which strengtheneth me…" (Philippians 4:13. All things include the keeping of His Sabbath commandment.

That is the reason for which our Savior came and died a most ignominious death. The angel comforts Joseph, "…Joseph, thou son of David, fear not to take unto thee Mary thy wife; for that which is conceived in her is of the Holy Ghost… and she shall bring forth a son, and thou shall call His name Jesus; for He shall save His people from their sins…" (Matthew 1:20, 21).

Jesus' mission is to restore us back to righteousness. He came to be the supreme example to all men who seek to be reunited with the God of creation. In the process He kept all of His Father's commandments. So must we who call upon His name and claim Him as our own.

That which was conceived of the Holy Ghost is divine. By His divinity He laid hold on the throne of God…by His humanity he touched humanity. As the son of man He taught us to obey. As the Son of God, He gave us the power to obey. Jesus did not come to save us in our sins. The angel reported to Joseph that He came to save us from our sins. He came that we may be righteous. That righteousness is exclusively available by faith in Jesus.

As a people seeking the heavenly kingdom, we must not only seek that kingdom by the words we speak; but our profession must be made manifest by a life of obedience to God's word. Such a life portrays a true connection to the Savior. It demonstrates our faith in Him. It is that faith which leads to righteousness.

That righteousness by faith is spoken of by the apostle Paul in these terms, "…Who through faith subdued kingdoms, wrought righteousness, obtained promises, stopped the mouths of lions… quenched the violence of fire, escaped the edge of the sword, out of weakness was made strong, waxed valiant in fight, turned to flight the armies of aliens… women received their dead raised to life again; and others were tortured, not accepting deliverance; that they might obtain a better resurrection…" (Hebrews 11:33-35). Such is the faith that produces righteousness.

God the Creator has never asked any man to do any task which he (man) is incapable of doing. When that man lays hold on God's word by faith, the impossible becomes possible. In fact, in the very command to perform the task, abides the divine power to accomplish it.

It is no different with God's blessed Sabbath-day. By faith in the God who gave it to you as a wonderful gift, you can keep God's Sabbath holy. By His grace, which He so freely imparts, you have the power to obey when He says, "…Remember the Sabbath Day to keep it Holy…" (Exodus 20:8).

Like our Redeemer, Jesus Christ, God wants us to keep His laws perfectly. That includes His Sabbath command. Paul writes to the church at Ephesus, "…For by grace are ye saved, through faith; and not of yourselves: it is the gift of God… not of works least any man should boast… for we are His workmanship, created in Christ Jesus unto good works, which God had before ordained that we should walk in them…" (Ephesians 2:8-10.

Not only are we saved by grace through faith, but we are called to righteousness through faith also. Paul concludes that the faith that saves us is the same faith we should employ in walking after good works, which is righteousness.

The acceptance of Jesus Christ by faith is our ticket to heaven. Living a righteous life by faith is our preparation for heaven. Sin, which is unrighteousness, will not inherit the kingdom of heaven. For this reason, Paul counsels his young minister Titus, "… For the grace of God that bringeth salvation hath appeared to all men… teaching us that denying ungodly lusts, we should live soberly, righteously and Godly, in this present life…looking for that blessed hope, and the glorious appearing of the great God and our Savior Jesus Christ…" (Titus 2:11-13).

The righteousness that comes by faith requires the keeping of God's law, which includes the Sabbath commandment. How can we be righteous if we neglect the only one that can make us righteous? Faith in Jesus Christ will lead the truly penitent and the seeker of truth to accept the gift of the Sabbath from the God of Creation. When we accept this gift, we are strengthened in our walk towards the heavenly kingdom.

The promise from God is this, "…Fear thou not for I am with you; be not dismayed, for I am your God; I will strengthen thee; yea I will help thee; yea I will uplift thee with the right hand of My righteousness…" (Isaiah 41:10).

The faith that pleases God is the faith that denies our own wishes and allows us to submit to what He requires. The faith that leads to righteousness is the faith that moved the Savior to exclaim, "…O My Father, if it be possible, let this cup pass from me: nevertheless, not as I will, but as thou wilt…" (Matthew 26:39).

As He faced the cross of Calvary, the horrors of His impending crucifixion became ever so real to Him. The Savior, though weak in his human flesh and unable to bear it, yet submitted to His Father's will. We must do likewise. Whatever the reasons or pretexts you choose, to not keep God's Sabbath-day holy, you must abandon them and submit to God's will. Our only obligation as children of God is to do His bidding. The wise man Solomon declares, "…Let us hear the conclusion of the whole matter: Fear God and keep His commandments, for this Is the whole duty of man…" (Ecclesiastes 12:13).

This is the promise for those who obey, "…Blessed are they that do His commandments, that they may have a right to the tree of life, and may enter in through the gates into the city…' (Revelation 22:14). For those that knowingly reject the Sabbath, here is the condemnation, "…For without are dogs, and sorcerers, and whoremongers, and murderers, and idolaters, and whosoever loveth and maketh a lie…" (Revelation 22: 15).

The people for whom Jesus will return will be a people, who by faith, have lived righteously. They would have, by His grace, kept all His commandments, including the Sabbath commandment. John the Revelator describes them thus, "…And to her(Christ's church) was granted that she should be arrayed in fine linen, clean and white: for the fine linen is the righteousness of saints..." (Revelation 19:8)

John concludes, "...Here is the patience of the saints: here are they that keep the commandments of God, and the faith of Jesus..." (Revelation 14:12)

Jesus asks: "...Will the Son of man find faith on the earth when He comes?..."   (Luke 18:8).

John assures us that He will. There will be a faithful people who will harken to God's word and, by faith, keep all His commandments, including the Sabbath commandment. The question is, will you be one of them?

You cannot have it any clearer than that. The Sabbath, God's special gift to His people, distinguishes them from the rest of all creation. The righteousness they receive is God's righteousness. It is obtainable only through uncompromising faith in His word. His word says, "...Remember the Sabbath-day to keep it holy..." (Exodus 20:8).

There may be some who may not agree with God's word. Others have twisted it to fit their particular theological perspective. That is not faith. It certainly is not God's righteousness.

The next chapter offers some thoughts, from the standpoint of God's word, on how to keep the Sabbath-day holy as God has commanded.

CHAPTER 13

Some Thoughts on Keeping The Sabbath Holy

Throughout this volume, Scriptural and historical evidence have been presented which demonstrate the validity, sacredness, and importance of the Seventh-day Sabbath in the life of the Christian and God's plan of redemption. In an attempt to share some thoughts on how one may keep the Sabbath holy, I would recap and expound on some of that evidence. All admonitions in this regard will be based solely on the word of God. They are not meant to be a legalistic body of rules and regulations; but rather, they are offered as sound Biblical principles which can be incorporated in one's desire and commitment to follow God's command to keep the Sabbath-day holy.

In dealing with this subject, the first thing one needs to remember is that no man can make the Sabbath-day holy. God has already done that from creation. Moses relates, "...And God blessed the seventh day, and sanctified it, because that in it he had rested from all His work which God created and made..."(Genesis 2:2).

There is nothing that we can do to make the Sabbath, or any other day for that matter, holy. God simply asks us to cooperate with His program. In order for us to cooperate with God, we must first believe God. We must have faith in His word. That faith, as was pointed out elsewhere in this volume, demands action on our part.

When we have that faith in God, then obeying Him, by doing what He asks us to do, would be no problem. In fact, obeying His command becomes joyful and delightful. So it must be with regard to God's Sabbath. It must first be settled in one's mind that the seventh day, now called Saturday, is indeed God's blessed Sabbath-day.

God's Sabbath is to man, a divine oasis in the immense sands of time which appears every seven days. Like the morning dew, it never fails to appear. As tired, weary souls, we can look forward to that oasis. We can be assured that we will find rest because the God of creation has ordained it thus. It is a place in time from which we rest from our labors. We should welcome it with joy, peace and a sense of holy fulfillment. More importantly, the Seventh-day Sabbath is an emblem of our spiritual rest in our Lord and Savior, Jesus Christ.

Not unlike the oasis to a weary, desert traveler, God's Sabbath provides a place of reflection, refreshment and rejuvenation. It is a place of rest and a time of repose. So God lovingly reminds us, "...Remember the Sabbath-day to keep it holy. Six days shalt thou labor and do all thy work. But the seventh day is the Sabbath of the Lord thy God. In it thou shalt not do any work, thou, nor thy son, nor thy daughter, nor thy manservant, nor thy maidservant, nor thy cattle, nor thy stranger that is within thy gates. For in six days the Lord made the heaven and the earth, the sea and all that in then is, and rested on the seventh day. Wherefore the Lord blessed the Sabbath-day and hallowed it...."(Exodus. 20:8-11).

From sunset on Friday to sunset on Saturday, we should refrain from our secular labors and commercial activity. Jeremiah warns us, "... Thus saith the Lord God; Take heed to yourselves, and bear no burden on the Sabbath-day nor bring it in by the gates of Jerusalem. Neither carry forth a burden out of your houses on the Sabbath-day neither do ye any work, but hallow ye the Sabbath-day, as I commanded your fathers (Jeremiah. 17:21-22).

The Sabbath should be a time of conscious, unbroken communion with God. It is a special time to contemplate His love and goodness towards us during the past six days. Through our many challenges, struggles and victories in those days, God has been with us. He desires to draw even closer to us on the Sabbath-day. The Sabbath is a time in which we pause to honor the Creator for His grace, mercy and manifold blessings towards us. It is a time that should be unencumbered by the many secular activities of our lives.

Before the Sabbath begins, time should be spent in preparation of clothing, food and the completion of household chores. Most importantly, our hearts must be in preparation to spend the sacred Sabbath hours with our Creator.

Hence Isaiah cautions us, "…If thou turn away thy foot from the Sabbath, from doing thy pleasure on My holy day; and call the Sabbath a delight the holy of the Lord, honorable, and shall honor Him, not doing thine own ways, nor finding thine own pleasure, nor speaking thine own words: then shalt thou delight thyself in the Lord: And I will cause thee to ride upon the high places of the earth, and feed thee with the heritage of Jacob thy father: for the mouth of the Lord hath spoken it…" (Isaiah 58: 13-14).

God's Sabbath is a time of prayer and holy communion with our Creator. Putting aside all worldly influences, pleasures and interests, one should focus one's thoughts, words and actions on matters that glorify God and uplift the Savior to our families and fellowman. As such, the Sabbath-day should begin with prayer and Bible reading. There is no better way to communion with our Maker than to begin the Sabbath-day with prayer and study of His word.

For families, the beginning of the Sabbath should be spent in family worship. The parents should lead out with prayers of thanksgiving. The children may join in with songs of praise and adoration to the One who created and redeemed them. All members of the family should thus recognize the One who has set apart this sacred time for undisturbed fellowship with Him. Words of testimony are perfectly appropriate for this time. Engaging the family in this manner, as the Sabbath draws near, demonstrates to God and to man that we honor the God of creation as the only true God. The rest of the evening may be spent in reading and meditation on the Sacred word or other spiritual literature. Listening to solemn, Christian music elevates the thoughts and directs the mind heavenward. This is a most fitting activity for Sabbath evening. It places the worshipper in the very presence of Almighty God.

If there is a most important activity in which to engage on

the Sabbath-day, it would be attending worship services at church. Moses instructs God's people, "...Six days should work be done, but the seventh day is the Sabbath of rest, an holy convocation (gathering): ye shall do no work therein. It is the Sabbath of the Lord in all your dwellings...:(Leviticus 23:3)

Our Lord and Savior, Jesus Christ, who is our example, lived in perfect harmony with this principle. The apostle Luke reports,"...And He (Jesus) came to Nazareth, where He had been brought up: and, as His custom was, He went into the synagogue on the Sabbath-day, and stood up for to read..." (Luke 4:16). Of course, the apostle Paul admonishes us, "...Not forsaking the assembling of ourselves together, as the manner as some do, but exhorting one another: and so much the more, as ye see the day approaching..." (Hebrews 10:25).

The Sabbath-day is the time in which God requires His people to gather together in public worship of Him. It is also a time, according to the apostle Paul, of sweet fellowship with those of like faith.

Spending some time in nature is a most profitable way in which to spend some of the Sabbath hours. The Savior challenges us, "...Consider the lilies of the field, how they grow; they toil not, neither do they spin..." (Matthew 6:28). The Savior was constantly directing the minds of His audience to nature and its lessons for our lives. The parables of the wheat and the tares, the sower and the seed and many other object lessons testify to the Savior's recognition of nature in the lives of His saints. The Psalmist David joins in unison, "...When I consider the heavens, the work of thy fingers, the moon and the stars, which thou hast ordained..." (Psalm 8:3).

To spend some time contemplating His creation is a wonderful way to honor the Creator on His blessed Sabbath-day. It is a marvelous time to reflect on God's great creations and appreciate His love and goodness towards us in creating them for us.

The Sabbath is a day on which to do good for others and be of service to our fellow man, particularly the less fortunate. The Lord of the Sabbath, when confronted with the issue of doing a good work on the Sabbath, responded to His opposition, "...How much then is a man better than a sheep? Wherefore it is lawful to do well on the Sabbath..."

(Matthew 12:12). Visiting the sick, feeding the poor and all other acts of mercy were deemed by Our Savior to be honorable activities to engage in on the Sabbath-day.

Before the Sabbath begins, we should endeavor to put away all differences, malice and prejudice between brethren and family. Bitterness and wrath should be expelled from the soul. Harboring such feelings impairs our communion with God. Thoughts of forgiveness and acts of love should envelop our person and permeate our minds. Practicing thus on the Sabbath-day will strengthen us to act similarly throughout the rest of the week. It will transform our characters to be more like Our Savior.

Good works, Christian fellowship, healthy thoughts, family and public worship and a trip into nature are all desirable activities in which we may engage on the Sabbath–day.

More important than what we do or do not do on the Sabbath-day, however, is our firm conviction that the seventh day, and not the first, is God's Holy Sabbath-day. If we hold that firm conviction and steadfast determination to follow God's command, He will lead us, through the power of His Holy Spirit, into all truth. He would direct our minds to the things we ought to do, say and engage in, on His holy Sabbath-day.

When that conviction is made and the determination is settled, God promises to bless us. Says He through His prophet Isaiah, "… Blessed is the man that doeth this, and the son of man that layeth hold on it; that keepeth the Sabbath from polluting it, and keepeth his hand from doing any evil…"(Isaiah 56:2). This is the promise of God. He not only created the Sabbath and gave it to man as an inestimable gift; God further declared blessings upon those who honor Him by keeping the Sabbath-day holy. Let no man deprive you of that precious promise and that invaluable gift.

The Sabbath is a recurring bookmark that shows up on every seventh page in the book of Salvation history. Some may deny it but no man can avoid it. Others may trample upon it, but God's blessings remain upon it. The archenemy may claim to change it, but God declares it immutable. His desire is for us to keep it holy.

Finally, it must be carefully noted, that the purpose of this volume is not to institute or order a set of rites, regulations and rituals in the mind of the reader. Rather, it is a frank attempt to illustrate the importance and blessings of obeying God in all aspects of our Christian experience, including the requirement to keep His Sabbath-day holy..

The Sabbath of the Ten Commandments not only warns of the danger that lies ahead; but offers some help in preparing us to face the unmitigated onslaught of the man of sin. Obedience is the highest form of praise. The wise man Solomon knew this well. He admonishes us, "...Let us hear the conclusion of the whole matter; fear God and keep His commandments; for this is the whole duty of man..." (Ecclesiastes 12:13). His commandments include keeping His Sabbath-day holy.

The greatest sin of the Jews of old was their rejection of the Messiah. Despite all the evidence available to them in their sacred writings, His very presence in their midst and the living testimonies of His disciples, His chosen people did not recognize and honor their Savior. They chose to follow their leaders rather than heed the word of God. They ultimately rejected and finally crucified Him.

The burdens of man-made rites and rituals that the leaders laid upon the Sabbath-day constituted their second greatest sin. The unscriptural litany of regulations, rites and rituals cast about the Sabbath-day led the people to feel that God's Sabbath was burdensome. Consequently, untold millions of His professed followers today have cast aside this most precious gift from the Creator.

Many Christians today, not unlike the Jews of old, are paying homage to their misguided religious leaders in trampling upon and casting aside God's holy Sabbath-day. So many are ignoring the plain teachings of Scripture and following men's tradition. They are heeding the false teachings and practices of men, thus rendering void the Commandments of God.

This is the greatest sin of Christendom. They are rejecting, by their actions in regard to the Sabbath-day, the God whom they profess to love.

When the Roman armies surrounded Jerusalem and struck with deadly force, only the ones who accepted the Messiah were saved from their merciless fury. Likewise, only those who honor and keep all of God's commandments, including His blessed Sabbath commandment, will be saved when Rome strikes her final, deadly blow, instituting her mark of authority, Sunday sacredness. God's true people will reject the anti-Christ's mark and hold fast to His seal, the seventh day Sabbath.

The greatest desire of God's heart is to save us. Jesus admonishes us, "...And this is life eternal, that they might know thee, the only true God, and Jesus Christ, whom thou hast sent..." (John 17:3). To keep the Sabbath-day holy, as God has commanded, is the final test of obedience for God's people in these end times. It is also the best opportunity one can have to know God. This is how Adam and Eve came to know Him. He still provides this special time for us to come apart from the cares of the world and get to know Him in a very special way.

This, ultimately, is the purpose for keeping the Sabbath-day holy. When this truth is settled in your heart, then the Holy Spirit, whose job it is to guide you into all truth (John 16:13), will confirm in you the things you ought to do on His blessed Sabbath-day.

Therefore, when the fury of Rome strikes once again, you can be protected by following Jesus in keeping holy His blessed Sabbath-day. John reminds us, "... These shall make war with the Lamb. And the Lamb shall overcome them; for He is Lord of lords and King of kings: and they that are with Him are called, and chosen and faithful..." (Revelation 17:14)

Conclusion

If you have read this far, then you must be acutely aware of the fact that there is a great controversy going on. The contest is not only for control your mind and your worship, but for the rulership of the universe. The conflict is between our Lord and Savior, Jesus Christ and His archenemy, satan, who is ultimately the antichrist.

This battle, which began in heaven, has continued for millennia here on earth. It is drawing to a swift conclusion in our time. The parties, Christ and satan, are each represented by their servants, in the personage of angels and humans.

The apostle John writes from Patmos, "...And there was war in heaven: Michael and His angels fought against the dragon; and the dragon fought against His angels...And prevailed not, neither was their place found anymore in heaven...And the great dragon was cast out, that old serpent, called the devil and satan, which deceiveth the whole world. He was cast out into the earth, and his angels were cast out with him... And the dragon was wroth with the woman, and went to make war with the remnant of her seed, which keep the commandments of God and have the testimony of Jesus Christ..." (Revelation 12:7-9,17).

In this battle, you are either on the side of the God of creation, or you are on the devil's side. There is no middle ground. At the center of the conflict is the matter of worship. The apostle Paul declares, "...know ye not, that to whom ye yield yourselves servants to obey, his servants ye are to whom ye obey: whether of sin unto death, or of obedience unto righteousness..." (Romans 6:16).

The issue, ultimately, is whether one chooses to obey the God of creation, or to obey a man who claims to be God. Each of us must make a decision as to whether to honor God's commandments, including His Sabbath commandment; or whether to serve the antichrist.

God says that His Sabbath-day is the seventh day of the week, today called Saturday. The antichrist, in its manifestation of

Roman Catholicism, says we should honor Sunday, the first day of the week. God gives us a free choice. He desires for us to choose Him. Nevertheless, He allows us to make our own choices.

The Sabbath is the test commandment. (Exodus 16:4) For the times in which we live, this is more true than ever before. It is the choice we must make. In a day and time when many are discovering that God's Ten Commandments are indeed to be kept, you must decide which day is God's holy Sabbath day.

Consider for a moment the fact that some of the greatest proponents of restoring God's Ten Commandments as the moral foundation of the nation, are the very ones who have long proclaimed that God's law was nailed to the cross. This poses a dilemma for many. But you need not be deceived or confused. God's requirements are clear…all ten of His commandments must be kept as He intended them to. There is but only one choice you need to make… choose God's way, all the way.

In this volume, we have clearly presented the evidence about God's Sabbath-day. The Biblical record, historical facts and prophetic utterances have been offered in support of God's blessed Sabbath-day. We have plainly shown who created the Sabbath, as well as who has attempted to change it.

In conclusion, we will recap and summarize the facts which will not only illuminate the truth about the Sabbath; but would also point to its dire importance and consequences for the times in which we live.

There are many today, in the Christian world, who claim to worship the Creator. However, their attitude in regard to this testing truth, does not match their verbal pronouncement. Jesus addresses this condition. He declares, "…Well hath Esaias prophesied of you hypocrites, as it is written, This people honoureth me with their lips, but their heart is far from me… howbeit in vain do they worship me, teaching for doctrines the commandments of men. Full well ye reject the commandment of God that ye may keep your own tradition…" (Mark 7:6,7,9).

No one can deny that this declaration perfectly describes Christendom today with regards to the Sabbath truth. Though many claim Jesus as their Lord and Savior, they reject His clear example and plain teaching on the matter of the Sabbath. Worse yet, they uplift in its place, the mark of allegiance of the man of sin. The Bible testimony and historical facts point undeniably to that man of sin as being the Roman pontiff.

Today, the pope's writings confirm that fact. The late Pope John Paul declared, "…The celebration of the Christian Sunday remain, on the threshold of the third millennium, an indispensable element of our Christian identity…" (Section 31, **Dies Domini**). He continued, "…Christians will naturally strive to ensure that civil legislation respect their right to keep Sabbath (Sunday) holy…"(section 67 ibid)

His successor, Benedict XVI has continued on the same path. The Guardian of London , England reports, "… At an outdoor mass attended by an estimated 200,000 people, he (Benedict XVI) called for the rediscovery of the religious meaning of Sunday as an antidote to the rampant consumerism and religious indifference that was making the modern world a spiritual desert…" All cardinals, archbishops, bishops and priests have followed their pontiff's lead. They have all arisen to trumpet the call for Sunday sacredness. The call is loud and clear not only for Roman Catholics, but for all people to honor Sunday as a sacred day. But this is contrary to the word of God. The question is, whom will you obey?

On one hand, God says, "…Remember the Sabbath day to keep it holy…six days shall thou labor and do all thy work, but the seventh day is the Sabbath-day of the Lord thy God…"(Exodus 20:8-9). Jesus further admonishes us, "…If you love me keep my commandments… "(John 14:15). He makes the loving appeal to His children, "…Come out of Her My people; lest ye partake of her sins and receive her plagues…" (Revelation 18:4). He also warns us, "… Fear God and give glory to Him for the hour of His judgment is come… and worship Him who made the heavens and seas and fountains of waters…" (Revelation 14:7).

On the other hand, Rome is calling. She calls for Christians to reject God and accept the rule of the pope. The pope sends out a decree, asserting to force Christians, through the power of the state, to honor and obey him by making Sunday holy.

Through many Biblically weak arguments, religious leaders are casting aside God's commands, whilst uplifting the tradition of Rome. We have looked at, dealt with and presented the gross falsity of those positions. Be it for financial gain, perceived peace or personal prestige, these leaders are leading untold millions to their eternal damnation by rejecting the God of creation, the only true God.

It is simply impossible to worship God without obeying His commandments. Any teaching, which causes men to abandon and disregard God's commandments, constitutes another Gospel. Such is not the Gospel of Salvation. One may claim to worship God; but when the Sabbath is rejected and the mark of the antichrist, Sunday, is uplifted, the as in fact rejecting the very God whom he claims to serve, whilst worshipping the antichrist, whom he pretends to reject.

Beyond the obvious exposition on the Sabbath in the story of creation, we saw that all of God's prophets held it in highest regard. In fact, in times of reformation, it was to the Sabbath that God's people were directed. There is not a single record in Scripture where God's people were called to abandon the Sabbath and in its place keep Sunday holy.

The greatest of all the prophets, Jesus Christ, never sanctioned Sunday sacredness or disregarded the Sabbath. In fact, He taught men how to keep His Sabbath Holy as His Father intended. The Scripture clearly shows that it was His custom to honor God's Sabbath. Jesus is the very personification of the law. That law includes the Sabbath commandment.

The apostles, after the death and resurrection of Jesus Christ, continued to be obedient to God by keeping the Sabbath-day holy. The disciples did not make another day holy. No man can make a day holy. It is only a holy God that can make a day holy. The day that the Creator God has made holy is the seventh day, not the first.

Therefore, regardless of what the Church of Rome may teach, demand or force; the only holy day is God's Sabbath-day, the seventh day of the week, today called Saturday.

As we looked at the demise and fall of the political Roman

empire, we discovered that true Christianity was amalgamated with the pagan practices of the Roman state. That amalgamation, initiated by Emperor Constantine, gave rise to that massive structure of deception and false religion called Catholicism. That system, which calls itself Christian, is anything but Christian.

The teachings, dogmas and doctrines of popery are almost exclusively non-Biblical and anti-Christian. Sunday sacredness is the most profound. She claims it as her mark of authority. Her teachings on the state-of-the dead, intercession of dead saints, forgiveness of sins by her priests, the worship of icons, images and relics are most adamantly condemned by Scripture. In fact, the second of God's holy commandments, which prohibits image worship, is completely removed from her teachings. This allows for the practice of image worship, which is at the very foundation of this system.

Her doctrine of salvation through the church and confession to her priests are in direct contradiction to the word of God. It is to this system and its leader, satan himself, that Christians give their worship when they exalt Sunday in the place of the Lord's Sabbath. Regardless of the pretext they choose, the result is the same, devil worship.

But the God of love does not condemn them. He offers them the truth as it is in Jesus. God offers pardon to those who would turn away from their error and come to worship Him in spirit and in truth. He offers forgiveness to those who turn away from their wicked ways, and purpose in their hearts to honor Him by keeping holy His blessed Sabbath-day.

God pleads with the rebellious, "...If my people which are called by my name, shall humble themselves and pray and seek my face, and turn from their wicked ways; then will I hear from heaven, and will forgive their sins, and heal their land..." (2 Chronicles 7:14).

The Creator sends out a love message to those who would listen and obey, "... Fear God and give glory to Him; for the hour of His judgment is come; and worship Him who made heaven, and earth, and the sea, and the fountains of waters..." (Revelation 14:7). God warns His people who are ignorantly caught up in this impious system, by name or by practice, "...Come out of her, my people, that ye be not partakers of her sins and that ye receive not her plagues..." (Revelation 18:4).

The God of Creation, who gave us the Sabbath as a gift and as a sign of our sanctification, allows us the right to choose according to the dictates of our consciences. Such also is the foundation of the American ideal.

The Church of Rome expresses great disdain for the principles of the United States Constitution which embodies that right to choose. She concludes, "...We will rule the United States, and lay them at the feet at the vicar of Christ, that he may put an end to their Godless system of education and impious laws of liberty of conscience which are an insult to God and man..." (**Fifty Years in the Church of Rome,** page 282, Charles Chiniquy)

Chiniquy continues, "... long before I was ordained a priest, I knew that my church (The Roman Catholic Church) was the most implacable enemy of the Republic (The United States of America). My professors of Philosophy, History and Theology had been unanimous in telling me that the principles and laws of the Church of Rome were absolutely antagonistic to the laws and principles which are the foundation stones of the constitution of the United States..." (**ibid**, page 203).

He goes on, "...The American Constitution leaves every man free to serve God according to the dictates of his own conscience; but the Church of Rome declares that no man has ever had such a right, and that the pope alone can know and say what man must believe and do...The constitution of the United States denies the right in anybody to punish another for differing from him in religion. But, the Church of Rome says that she has the right to punish, with the confiscation of goods, or the penalty of death, those who differ in faith from the pope... "(**ibid**, page 284).

The U.S. Constitution, with its inherent principles of civil and religious liberties is an abhorrence to popery. The Papacy's longstanding position is that of hatred for the concepts of liberty and freedom that have found their finest hour in the American experience.

Pope Pius VII exclaimed, "...It was declared that all religious persuasions should be free and their worship publicly exercised. But, we have rejected this article as contrary to the canons and councils of the first Catholic Church..." (**Encyclical,** 1808).

The famous poet and eminent statesman, Lafayette, knew well the aims of popery for the United States of America. He traveled extensively throughout Europe and gathered much first hand information in that regard. He warned his contemporaries, "...If the liberties of the American people are ever destroyed, they will fall at the hands of the Catholic clergy..."

Ironically, President George W. Bush has made the accommodation of the Papacy, the hallmark of his presidency. Knowingly or unknowingly, the president is moving the country steadily towards papal rule. Since his inauguration as president in January 2000, George W. Bush has, seemingly oblivious to the aims of Rome, fashioned himself the champion and cheerleader of popery to the American people. He has visited, counseled with and established formidable alliances with leading Cardinals, Archbishops and Bishops in the United States. President Bush has dedicated a monument in the nation's capital to the honor of Pope John Paul II. In his dedication remarks, where he was surrounded by the crème de la crème of popery in the U.S., the President urged the nation to follow the teachings of Pope John Paul II. The late Pope John Paul II responded with great jubilation, "...We will come to view this as our little Vatican in the United States..."

To most Americans, this seems commendable and laudable. But, to many, it is immensely disturbing and disheartening. America was born as a Protestant nation. We are supposed to be protesting against the errors of Romanism. As a Protestant people, we should be holding fast to the Bible and the Bible only. Romanism and Americanism cannot exist side by side. One has to obliterate the other. The sad commentary is that whilst this sentiment is well understood by the agents of Rome, it is distant to most Americans. This is a simple fact of life which most seem not to realize. To follow the pope of Rome is tantamount to rejecting the word of God.

The type of activity engaged in by the president, coupled with legislation such as Homeland Security, The Patriot Act and Faith Based Initiative, constitute the fulfilling of the Biblical prophecy of the formation of the image of the beast. (Revelation 13).

What we are experiencing in America today is not security of the homeland, patriotic awakening or religious compassion; but rather, a rapid though stealthy implementation of papal rule. Papal rule is antagonistic to the American system of justice and liberty for all.

Under the right set of circumstances, most likely characterized by confusion and chaos, the papal solution of Sunday sacredness will be proposed. The evidence suggests that such is already the case. According to God's word, Sunday sacredness will be legislated and ultimately implemented. The citizenry, having disconnected themselves from God, by rejecting His Holy Sabbath-day, will force their petitions for Sunday sacredness. They will see it as a panacea for America's and the world's problems. Moves in that direction are well under way.

The people of God will surely then have to choose. Ellen White again writes, "…The Romish Church now presents a fair front to the world, covering with apologies her record of horrible cruelties. She has clothed herself in Christ- like garments; but she is unchanged. Every principle of popery that existed in past ages exists today. The doctrines devised in the darkest ages are still held. Let none deceive themselves. The popery that Protestants are now so ready to honor is the same that ruled the world in the days of Reformation, when men of God stood up, at the peril of their lives to expose her iniquities. She possess the same pride and arrogant assumption that lorded it over kings and princesses and claimed the prerogatives of God…" (**The Great Controversy**, page 571).

There is but one earthly power that has warred continuously against God since the first advent of our Savior. First, it attempted to kill the baby Jesus. It failed. Then it crucified the Savior. And again it failed; for the Lord rose on the first day of the week, three days after he was crucified. After Jesus' ascension to His Father, that warring power unleashed a reign of terror and torture on His followers. Rather than eradicating His name from the earth, her persecution was the fuel that ignited and spread the fire of the Gospel.

Unable to thwart the power of God's message of Salvation, they pretended to join Him. They mixed their false concepts of religion with the pure treasure of the Gospel. For a time, it seemed as though they would succeed in obliterating the true knowledge of God from the minds of the people. But, again they failed. God had raised up the Reformers who pointed men and women away from her deceptive heresies, to faith in a crucified and risen Savior.

Though that earthly power appeared to lose its might, it has resurrected and returned with a face more deceptive than ever before in its history. It openly claims to represent God, whilst at the same time working to usurp His position of Lord in the hearts of mankind. It presents a face of piety and goodwill as a cover for its insatiable appetite for ultimate power and control.

This entity is the Roman power. First, it ruled in its pagan form. Now it is prepared to dominate in its papal form. Many are deceived and are thus captivated by its frontal appeal of love and unity of all mankind. But beneath that velvet glove of love and unity is an iron hand of cruelty and despotism more sinister and more intolerant than any the world has ever seen.

It seeks nothing less than replacing God as the ruler of the universe. It covets the prerogatives of God. Foremost among the prerogatives of God that the Romish church has claimed, is her authority to transfer the sanctity of the seventh day of the week to the first. It is waging a secret, yet effective and unrelenting war to take the seat of God. Its true purpose and character will soon be made manifest to a stunned on-looking world.

As a child of the God of creation, you don't have to be deceived, surprised or afraid. In this final conflict, all the world is involved. There is but one of two choices to make. One must choose either the Mark of the Beast, Sunday Sacredness, or the Seal of God, His Holy Sabbath-day.

By faith, the true followers of God will choose His Sabbath and strive, by His grace, to keep it holy. Through deception or willing ignorance, most will unfortunately choose the Mark of the Beast.

To receive God's seal is to settle in one's mind the eternal and enduring nature of His moral law, which has the Sabbath commandment as its seal. That law is for all men in all ages. Contrary to Jewish tradition and popular belief, the Sabbath is not characterized by an endless series of rites and rituals. It is not a man-made collection of do's and don'ts.

The Sabbath experience is a commemoration of God's love for us in providing all that we need in this life and throughout eternity. It is a call for sinful man to remember the creative and redemptive power of an Almighty God.

Sabbath keeping is an outworking of our saving relationship with God, through His Son Jesus Christ. It is not a denominational or religious dogma. Observing the Sabbath is evidence of a person's true sanctification by the God who created him.

The acceptance and keeping of the Lord's Sabbath is a believer's supreme act of faith. It is an open demonstration of one's trust in the God who created the world and redeemed fallen man from sin. The giving of the Sabbath by God at creation remains the irrefutable foundation of our Christian experience.

The Sabbath provides for total and complete surrender to God. Unlike any other day of the week, the Sabbath-day serves not only as a sign of the Christian's sanctification, but it is also a mark of separation between those who serve the God of creation and those who serve Him not. The Sabbath exemplifies a unique relationship between the Creator God and His supreme creation, man.

God declares it to be a sign of deliverance. To the Jews, He proclaimed,"...And remember that thou wast a servant in the land of Egypt and that the Lord thy God brought thee out thence through a mighty hand and by a stretched out arm: therefore the Lord thy God commanded thee to keep the Sabbath holy..." (Deuteronomy 5:15)

Likewise today, when by faith, we are delivered from sin by the grace of God through the blood of His Son, Jesus, we too are commanded to keep the Sabbath-day holy.

The commandments include the Sabbath commandment. One does not keep the law, including the Sabbath to be saved. The law, including the Sabbath commandment, should be kept because you are saved. It is a matter of being, not doing. Law abiding Christians are the greatest evidence of the Christian faith.

The apostle Paul concurs, "...For he spake in a certain place of the seventh day on this wise and God did rest on the seventh day from all His works...For if Jesus had given them rest, then would He not afterward have spoken of another day...there remaineth therefore a rest for the people of God ... For he that has entered into His rest, He also hath ceased from his own works, as God did from His..." (Hebrews 4:4,8-10).

God's seventh-day Sabbath is not an attempt at good works; but rather a rest from evil works. This is what Jesus offers us. When we accept Him, we follow Him by doing what God says we ought to do. We cannot make the Sabbath-day holy by our works, but rather we show our obedience to God by cooperating with Him in resting from our labors on the seventh-day. To do so requires an abiding faith in the Creator who made the Sabbath holy.

In the process of keeping the Sabbath-day holy, we are reminded of a God who created time and gives us a piece of it. Keeping the Sabbath holy is the supreme act of faith and loyalty to the God of creation. It points one in the direction of the origin of his faith. The Sabbath reminds us of what God declared and Moses recorded, "...In the beginning God created ..." (Genesis 1:1).

As a Christian, the question is not whether God's Sabbath is still binding; but rather, do you have enough faith in the God who created you and the Sabbath. Further, the question is posed, Do you have faith enough to obey God's command rather than man's traditions?

Times of fear and uncertainty produce religious zealotry. We are living in such a time. But religious zealotry is no substitute for a sanctified heart, evidenced by an obedient spirit. Sabbath keeping is verily the sign of true obedience and sanctification.

As you settle in your heart the question of keeping God's Sabbath, you must follow Jesus. He is your supreme example. You must heed the teachings of the prophets as to what you need to do to comply with God's requirements to keep the Sabbath-day holy. God promises a blessing for those who accept the Sabbath truth.

In a cartoon by the famous cartoonist, Bruce Beattie, which appeared In the Daytona Beach News Journal on March 15th, 2004, a message of prophetic proportions was delivered. Below a caricature of President George W. Bush standing at a the presidential podium and holding a document in his hand, the following copy appeared,

"... Here's one my conservative base is REALLY going to like. A constitutional amendment requiring folks to attend church on Sundays..."

Considering the political influence of the president's conservative base and their new found zeal for bringing back the Ten Commandments as the moral foundation of the nation, it won't be very long before the issue of which day is the true Sabbath comes to the forefront. Couple this with the fact that we now have a majority Roman Catholic Supreme Court, a Roman Catholic Attorney General and a plethora of devout Roman Catholics in all positions of power and influence in our government, Bruce Beattie's cartoon doesn't seem so cartoonish. It speaks so pointedly to the political reality of the day. Mr. Beattie's cartoon was verily a prophetic glimpse of things to come.

When the Sabbath question becomes more manifest as the testing issue in the conflict between Christ and satan, all will have to make a choice. Each choice has vital consequences. To choose the mark of apostasy (Sunday sacredness) is to disconnect oneself from the creator. The consequence will be to suffer God's wrath when Jesus returns. John the Revelator declares, "...And the beast was taken and with him the false prophet that wrought miracles before him, with which he deceived them that had received the mark of the beast, and them that worshipped the image. These both were cast alive into the lake of fire burning with brimstone..." (Revelation 19:20).

But, of those that keep God's Sabbath, thus receiving His seal, John writes, "...Here is the patience of the saints, here are they that keep the commandments of God and the faith of Jesus.... And God shall wipe away all tears from their eyes. And there shall be no more death, neither sorrow, nor crying, neither shall there be anymore pain for the former things are passed away..." (Revelation 14:12; 21:4).

Finally, Isaiah declares, "...For as the new heavens and the new earth, which I will make, shall remain before me, saith the Lord, so shall your seed and your name remain... And it shall come to pass, that from one new moon to another, and from one Sabbath to another, shall all flesh come to worship before me, saith the Lord..." (Isaiah 66:22,23).

The truth about the Sabbath is that is was instituted by God at

CONCLUSION

creation. It was preached by the prophets and practiced by Jesus. The Sabbath was honored by the apostles and revered by the early church.

The Sabbath was lost sight of for a period of time during the dark ages of Roman Catholic apostasy, when the Bible was taken away from the people. God is, in these times, revealing His Sabbath truth to His people. When all is over in this present world, and Jesus comes to make all things new, the promise is that His followers will keep the Sabbath in honor of His creative and redemptive work in our lives.

The same God who created the heavens, the earth, and all that are in them, and rested on the seventh-day; is the same God who recreated us when we submitted or lives to Him by faith in Jesus Christ.

The Sabbath is His sign of creation, redemption and sanctification. To observe God's seventh-day Sabbath is to truly show the world that you carry the blood stained banner of Prince Immanuel. He created the world and all that is in it. He then gives us the Sabbath as and eternal reminder of who He is. That is the truth about the Sabbath.

Today, you must decide whose side you're on. Your decision on the Sabbath will determine where you'll spend eternity. It will be either with the God of creation or with the man of perdition. **Understanding the Sabbath of the Ten Commandments** will help you to make the right decision.

May God guide you in making that decision.